Ramya Nagesh is a barrister at No 5 Chambers who specialises primarily in criminal law. She has a particular interest in cases involving a hate crime element: as well as appearing in those cases for both the Prosecution and the Defence, she also sits as the independent legal representative on the West Midlands Hate Crime Panel. Ramya has authored articles about hate crime for the legal publications "Criminal Law and Justice Weekly" and "Counsel".

Over the years, then, Ramya has built a wealth of expertise in criminal matters, for both the Prosecution and the Defence, representing both individuals and corporations. The vast majority of her work is in the Crown Court, where her practice is in all areas of general crime, but she also appears in the Court of Appeal. She advises a variety of clients on a range of matters, including international human rights law, appeals to the Court of Appeal (including in Imprisonment for Public Protection cases) and appeals to the Criminal Cases Review Commission.

As well as her daily work in Court, Ramya has worked on larger Inquests and Inquiries. For example, she was one of a team representing an interested party to the Hillsborough Inquest in 2014. She was also instructed in a similar role for a party to the Independent Jersey Care Inquiry that year, which examined allegations of decades of physical and sexual abuse of children in the Jersey care system.

A Practical Guide to the Law in Relation to Hate Crime

A Practical Guide to the Law in Relation to Hate Crime

Ramya Nagesh
Barrister (Lincoln's Inn),
LLB (Hons), MSc (LSE)

Law Brief Publishing

Published 2020 by Law Brief Publishing, an imprint of Law Brief Publishing Ltd
30 The Parks
Minehead
Somerset
TA24 8BT

www.lawbriefpublishing.com

Paperback: 978-1-912687-65-7

To my parents, sister and brother-in-law, for being a better family than I could have ever wished for

To my partner Andrew, for being my rock in many ways that I cannot describe, and for keeping me company into the early hours when I was writing and re-writing this book

And to Ollie and Rupert, despite the fact that they will never read this book, unless the education of cats takes a rapid turn

PREFACE

It may seem odd, at first, to use the word 'hate' to describe an area of the criminal law. After all, 'hate' is an emotive word, perhaps one of the most emotive in the English language. It seems out of place in the legal world, which generally can be said to place reason above emotion. Consider the law of hate crime further, though, and it becomes clear that label is the only one that makes sense. The very purpose of hate crime law is to target something that is inextricably linked with high-running emotion: the most hostile manifestations of prejudice. In this way, then, it is different from much of the criminal law. The criminal law is largely concerned only with the action of the offender and shows interest in the mind only insofar as to establish the requisite intent. Hate crime law, however, goes one step further and considers whether prejudice is involved – whether the offender's actions were motivated by prejudice, or demonstrate prejudice. In a habitual criminal case, motive is irrelevant to an offender's guilt or innocence. In a hate crime case, motive can make all the difference.

Hate crime offences themselves are not a new phenomenon; history is littered with examples of horrific crimes fuelled by prejudicial views. By contrast, the current law of hate crime has only emerged over the last few decades. Despite its relatively short lifespan, however, it has already mushroomed – from a handful of specific offences focused upon racial hostility to an entire statutory regime which protects victims of hostility due to their race, religion, sexual orientation, transgender identity or disability.

Whether you are a practitioner, student or academic, then, an understanding of the law in relation to hate crime is immensely useful. This book is intended to provide you with such an understanding. It is by no means a detailed philosophical analysis of hate crime; rather, it is a practical guide to assist all who wish to navigate this rather unique, and sometimes complicated, area of law.

You will see that the book is set out in the following way: a history of hate crime, an overview of the law, an analysis of key concepts, a detailed analysis of the law and a practitioner's toolkit. With this combination of chapters, the book will be suitable for both detailed study and as a quick reference point when acting in a hate crime case.

As ever, the law is continually evolving. I therefore make clear that the law in this book is correct as at 28th February 2020.

Ramya Nagesh
February 2020

CONTENTS

CHAPTER ONE
A HISTORY OF HATE AND THE LAW

This chapter is a history of hate and the law in the United Kingdom. It focuses on hate based upon race, religion, sexual orientation, gender identity and disability, to reflect the areas that the criminal law addresses today.

On what we might allow ourselves to imagine was a balmy Grecian day over two thousand years ago, Aristotle penned his thoughts about the impact of a country's climate on the character of its inhabitants. So it was that people of a cold country, particularly in Europe, apparently lacked skill and intelligence as a consequence of their harsh conditions, but possessed spirit. The former hampered their political development, yet the latter allowed them to remain free. People in often hot regions of Asia, according to Aristotle, had the opposite problem: they had much skill and intelligence, but lacked spirit of character. So it was that they would be condemned to a state of slavery and servitude. It was the Greek people who were perfectly placed geographically, in Aristotle's assessment, and so it followed that they possessed an ideal combination of both spirit and intelligence.

Basing our judgment of a person on the country in which they are raised may seem to have little place in modern discourse. However, these words of the ancient philosopher echo ideas that have found themselves resurrected in various forms throughout the ages. It seems that throughout history, we have confronted those who are markedly different from us in appearance, background, sexual orientation, gender identity or physical or mental disability by presuming they possess an innate set of personal characteristics. All too often, these presumed characteristics have been used to justify the seizure of power, the oppression of an entire group, and the deprivation of liberty. So it is that we have, in our history of humanity, witnessed slavery, colonialism, laws criminalising homosexual relationships, violence against strangers, discrimination (explicit and implicit) at the workplace, inequal legal partnership rights, hate-fuelled vandalism and much more.

You may wonder why a practical guide to the current law on hate crime would begin with a chapter about the history of hate. The reason is this: the law of hate crime is relatively young. The evil it seeks to tackle is, by comparison, a Goliath; prejudice and discrimination have existed in one form or another for many centuries. It is arguably impossible to extract the present from its past. For example, the racial, homophobic or otherwise prejudicial slur might sound simply like an unpleasant word to those of us unaffected directly by it. To the person at whom it is directed, it may carry resounding echoes of centuries of subjugation, carving into deep wounds. The person uttering the words may appear to simply be reaching for a curse in the heat of the moment. However, that person is resurrecting language used for generations to crush and subjugate an entire group of people. Hate Crime offences carry a whole history with them. As practitioners, it can only help us to understand something of that history.

It would be possible to fill an entire book with the history of hate crime, and so it has been necessary to streamline this chapter. I have focused on the following categories of discrimination: a) race and religion; b) sexual orientation and gender identity; c) discrimination on the grounds of disability. The choice of these headings is simply to reflect the groups explicitly set out in hate crime legislation. It is not to deliberately exclude or ignore the struggles that have been faced by other groups, such as women or the elderly.

Race and Religion

In the United Kingdom, the migration of Jewish settlers from France after the Norman Conquest of 1066 is perhaps one of the earliest, clear examples of hostility towards an entire racial group. By the mid 12th Century, vitriol spread throughout the country, with the Christian population accusing the Jewish people of heinous acts, including the sacrificial murder of Christian children. As unbelievable as such accusations sound to us in the 21st Century, these dangerous whispers only served to strengthen anti-Jewish feeling.

One of the starkest illustrations of this rife anti-Semitism is the mass suicide in York in the year 1190. There had been ever-growing hostility towards the Jewish population, anger at the taxes used to fund the crusades and resentment at the presence of Jewish people at the coronation of Richard I, which had led to riots during the coronation itself. Matters reached boiling point when a fire in the City of York led to chaos and looting throughout the City. The City's Jewish people fled to the 'King's Tower', inside the castle. However, a mob of angry citizens surrounded the tower, joined by troops. The occupants attempted to hold them back, by pelting them with stones, but (according to various accounts) realised that they could not hold themselves out against their attackers for much longer. Rather than suffer the potential horrors awaiting them, they decided to meet death together. The father of each family killed his wife and children, and then himself; some accounts suggest that there were about 150 people who died in this manner.

Such stories of human tragedy do not appear to have quashed anti-Semitic action. About 100 years later (in 1290) Edward I issued an Edict of Expulsion, which led to Jewish people being excluded from the United Kingdom until 1656.

When we leap forward to the 15th Century, we see the European colonial project, spreading a concept of 'racial hierarchy' that suited the agenda of the Colonisers. Thus the myth was perpetuated that native black and Asian people, for example, were inferior in every way to the white Europeans who violently took charge of their lands. The leader of the 1904 British Invasion of Tibet, Sir Francis Younghusband, illustrates this attitude perfectly in the following passage in *The Heart of a Continent:*

> "*No European can mix with non-Christian races without feeling his moral superiority over them. He feels, from the first contact with them, that whatever may be their relative positions from an intellectual point of view, he is stronger morally than they are. And facts show that this feeling is a true one. It is not because we are any cleverer than the natives of India, because we have more brains or bigger heads than they have, that we rule India; but because we are stronger morally than they are. Our superiority over them is not due to mere sharpness of intellect, but to that higher moral nature which we have attained in the development of the human race.*[1]"

The 17th and 18th Centuries saw young black and Asian people being used as slaves, prostitutes, performers, servants and nannies in the United Kingdom. Many were forcibly brought to the country. Although the trade in slaves formally ended by the Abolition of the Slave Trade Act 1807, that certainly did not spell the end of subjugation of those native to the Colonies.

The British rule over its colonies was to crumble and fall by the mid 20th Century. As the dust settled, however, it became apparent that it left behind the impact of centuries of prejudice, and attitudes towards 'foreigners' that would not be easily extinguished.

The 1950s and 1960s saw a flow of immigration, with large numbers of people arriving from India. There was a spike between 1965 and 1972, when Ugandan dictator Idi Amin made a sudden, brutal decision to expel all 50,000 Gujarati Indians from Uganda. Around 30,000 emigrated to the UK. The experience of many of those immigrants was to meet open hostility and discrimination. Landlords would not rent them

---

1 F.E.Younghusband, *The Heart of a Continent: A Narrative of Travels in Manchuria, Across the Gobi Desert, Through the Himalayas, the Pamirs and Chitral* (1896), 3rd Edition, pp.396 to 397

properties, signs declaring "No dogs, no blacks" were not uncommon, there was a perception that black and Asian people were 'dirty' and some claimed that immigrants liked to eat cat and dog food rather than meat aimed at humans. The 1964 Smethwick election in the Midlands region is remembered for the fact that Conservative MP Peter Griffiths won with the slogan: "*If you want a n***er for a neighbour, vote Liberal or Labour.*" Only four years later, MP Enoch Powell was to make the now infamous anti-immigration 'Birmingham Speech' – later to be dubbed the 'Rivers of Blood' speech.

There was, however, positive movement too. The Race Relations Act 1965 was the first piece of legislation to address the prohibition of racial discrimination. It banned racial discrimination in public places, and made the promotion of hated on the grounds of colour, race, or ethnic or national origins, an offence. Three years later, the Race Relations Act 1968 was passed to extend the prohibition of discrimination to apply to employment, housing and advertising. It was later superseded by the Race Relations Act 1976.

However, the 1970s and 1980s were dark times in Britain, particularly for those in the less financially stable strata, and did nothing to appease racial hostility. These two decades saw the establishment and growth of the violent 'National Front' – a group who believes in a concept of racial hierarchy (which sees racially white groups at the top), and promotes the conspiracy theory that non-white people were intentionally encouraged to migrate to Britain in order to breed with the indigenous inhabitants and thus bring about 'white genocide'.

The bubbling pot boiled over in the early 1980s, when a series of riots broke out in areas of London that had substantial African-Caribbean populations, such as Brixton, Wandsworth and Tottenham. These were generally sparked by protests against a specific police action in those areas but quickly became a method of venting a far deeper sense of injustice amongst the non-white population.

Race Relations in the United Kingdom in the 1990s and 2000s may be best characterised by a single name: Stephen Lawrence. The murder of this black teenager, waiting at a bus stop with a friend in 1993, was to spark protest, campaigns and arguably what became one of the most significant Judicial Inquiries in terms of race relations in the United Kingdom.

On the night of 22 April 1993, 18-year-old Stephen Lawrence was standing at a bus stop with his friend, Duwayne Brooks, when he was brutally stabbed in an unprovoked attack by a group of white youths. Brooks managed to get away from the attack, but Lawrence was killed. There was a police investigation, which led to the arrest of three young men; however, charges were dropped due to lack of evidence. The Senior Investigating Officer is said to have made a statement indicating that Duwayne Brooks could not be sure of his identification. Brooks has denied ever saying this. The family brought a private prosecution but this was halted when the Judge ruled that Brooks' identification evidence was inadmissible. The coroner's Inquest in 1997 recorded a verdict of unlawful killing in an unprovoked racist attack by five youths, and the Lawrence family lodged a formal complaint with the Police Complaints Authority about the standard of the police investigation.

In the Summer of 1997 the Home Secretary, Jack Straw, met Stephen Lawrence's parents; following this, the Home Office announced a judicial inquiry into the murder, to be led by retired High Court Judge, Sir William Macpherson. In December of that same year, a Police Complaints Authority report was released, finding that there were weaknesses, omissions and lost opportunities in the investigation, but no evidence of racist conduct by the police.

However, in February 1999, the MacPherson report was released. It found the police guilty of mistakes and – famously – found that there was institutional racism within the police force. It made seventy recommendations on changes to policing and public policy, as well as advising strengthening the Race Relations Act. In the year 2000, then, a new iteration of the Race Relations Act came into force, which placed a duty on specified public authorities to work towards the elimination of unlawful discrimination and to promote equality.

Finally, in November 2011, two of the original suspects (Dobson and Norris) for the Stephen Lawrence murder faced trial at the Central Criminal Court. The evidence heard by the jury included Lawrence's blood being found on Dobson's jacket, Lawrence's hair found in Norris' bag, and covert video evidence from the 1990s in which Norris talked about 'skinning' black people and setting them alight. The two were convicted in January 2012, almost twenty years after committing the murder. These convictions were not only significant for bringing justice to the Lawrence family, but also marked the climax to a tumultuous period in which the highest institutions in the country were forced to face the question of race relations in Britain.

Sexual Orientation and Gender Identity

It may be fair to say that recognition of the equal rights deserved by transgender people and by those of all sexual orientations has only found firm footing over the last 20 years, since the dawn of the new Millennium. Discrimination on the grounds of sexual orientation finds its roots not only in society, but in our legislation itself. The Buggery Act of 1552 made homosexuality a crime punishable by death. This law stayed part of the fabric of the United Kingdom for three centuries, until section 15 of the Offences Against the Person Act 1828 came into force. That section, however, simply replaced the 16th Century offence. Those convicted of sodomy faced imprisonment, the Pillory or death by hanging.

There are fewer clear records about the actions of, and attitudes towards, transgender people during this time period. It is known that in 1394, police arrested a male bodied sex worker who wore women's clothing and used the name 'Eleanor Rykener'. Rykener, who also found some employ as an embroideress, was arrested for performing a sex act with a man and was interrogated about two offences: prostitution and sodomy.

It was not until 1861 that capital punishment was abolished for the crime of buggery. The Offences Against the Person Act 1861 retained the crime, but the punishment was now imprisonment. Only twenty years later, section 11 of the Criminal Law Amendment Act 1885 extended the laws regarding homosexuality to include any kind of sexual activity between males. Interestingly, sexual activity between females was never acknowledged by the legislation. In 1895, the legendary author Oscar Wilde famously faced trial after the details of his affair with a British aristocrat were made public.

We move into the mid-Twentieth Century, and the year 1946 saw the first sex reassignment phalloplasty in Britain being performed, by one surgeon on another. However, in general, change in terms of homosexual or transgender issues was slow. Homosexual acts were still being criminalised, and we see little by way of open recognition of transgender issues. In 1952, for example, the pioneering computer scientist, mathematician and war-time code-breaker Alan Turing was convicted of 'gross indecency' for his relationship with 19 year-old Arnold Murray. His choice of punishment was either imprisonment, or probation. The latter, though, was conditional on his agreement to undergo hormonal treatment to reduce his libido. Faced with an arguably impossible choice, Turing opted for the hormonal treatment.

Not only were homosexual men targeted by the criminal law, those homophobic people who sought to take the law into their own hands might find themselves escaping a just punishment. For example, on 31 July 1950, 37 year-old English schoolteacher Kenneth Crowe was found viciously beaten and strangled to death in his home in Rotherham. He was wearing his wife's clothes and a wig. It transpired that he had approached a man named John Cooney who, discovering that

Crowe was a male, murdered him. Cooney was acquitted of murder and instead served only five years' imprisonment for manslaughter.

It was not until the 1960s that some positive movement was achieved. In 1965, Conservative peer Lord Arran proposed the decriminalisation of homosexual acts in the House of Lords. One year later, Humphrey Berkeley followed suit in the House of Commons. Despite being defeated, Labour MP Leo Abse took up the mantle and the Sexual Offences Bill was put before Parliament to address the issue.

This decade also saw some movement in terms of recognition of transgender issues. In 1961, English model April Ashley was revealed to be transgender. She is one of the earliest Britons known to have had sex reassignment surgery.

Thus was borne the Sexual Offences Act 1967. This decriminalised buggery and 'indecency' between men where three conditions were fulfilled: (i) the act had to be consensual; (ii) the act had to take place in private; (iii) the act had to involve only people that had attained the age of 21.

Although this was, in many ways, a landmark piece of legislation for the homosexual community, there was still a stark lack of equality with heterosexual people. For example, the age of consent to take part in homosexual activity was 21 years of age under this Act; the age of consent for heterosexual acts was 16. In addition, 'in private' was interpreted strictly by the courts. It was deemed to exclude acts taking place in a hotel, or in homes where a third person was present (even if in a different room). Additionally, it did not apply to Scotland, Northern Ireland, the Channel Islands or the Isle of Man, where all homosexual activity remained illegal.

Homosexual activities (within certain specified conditions) may have been decriminalised, but that did not mean that homosexual men were free to enjoy the social acceptance and freedom of their heterosexual counterparts. Homosexual men were still the subject of ridicule, prejudice and violence.

However, in 1988, the law took a leap backwards with the enactment of Section 28 of the Local Governments Act 1988. This law stated that a Local Authority should not: a) intentionally promote homosexuality or publish material with the intention of promoting homosexuality; b) promote the teaching in any maintained school of the acceptability of homosexuality as a pretended family relationship. The result was that children, from the youngest age, were given no positive messages about homosexuality. Teachers' weaponry for tackling homophobic bullying was substantially reduced; how could they penalise a student for shouting homophobic slurs at another without being accused of teaching the acceptability of homosexuality?

Matters began to bubble over towards the end of 1989, and six dark months during which a number of homosexual men were brutally murdered. In September 1989, a barrister called Christopher Schiliach was stabbed to death in his own home. He had been stabbed over forty times. Only one month later, a hotel porter named William Dalziel was found unconscious on the side of a road, suffering severe head injuries that would ultimately prove fatal. In April 1990, the actor Michael Boothe was found clinging to park railings, saying that he had been attacked by a group of six men. He later died from internal bleeding. His murder remains unsolved.

These bloody months sparked an emotional, powerful retaliation in July 1990. Hundreds of homosexual men and women marched from the park in which Boothe had been murdered to Ealing town hall, where they held a candlelit vigil. In addition, 'OutRage' was born: a campaign group that was to last until 2011. This group called for the police to start protecting gay men, rather than criminalising them. The Lesbian and Gay Police Association was formed in September 1990.

Conservative MP Edwina Currie raised the issue in Parliament in February 1994, when she proposed an amendment to the Criminal Justice and Public Order Bill to equalise the age of consent as between same sex and heterosexual activities. Her amendment was defeated by 370 votes to 280. Sir Anthony Durant subsequently proposed another amendment lowering the age of consent in homosexual activities to 18 years of age. That passed, with supporters including Michael Howard and John Major.

The European Court of Human Rights had its say in its decision of *Sutherland v United Kingdom* (1997). It found that Articles 8 (right to private life) and 14 (Protection from Discrimination) were violated by a discriminatory age of consent. By way of response, the UK Government assured the Court that it would propose a bill to Parliament for a reduction of the age of consent for homosexual acts from 18 to 16 years of age. It was still to be some time before the proposed change was realised, however; it was the Sexual Offences (Amendment) Act 2000 that lowered the age of consent to 16 years of age. It also finally recognised female homosexuality, introducing an age of consent for sexual acts between women.

On 18 September 2003 the Local Government Act 2003 was enacted, and the controversial section 28 (which had banned the promotion of homosexuality by Local Authorities) was removed. On 1 May 2004, the Sexual Offences Act 2003 came into force. That finally dissolved all previous sex-specific legislation and introduced offences that did not pay different regard to homosexual and heterosexual acts. So it was that true legislative equality for sexual acts between people of the same sex was not achieved until the dawn of the new Millennium.

Meanwhile, transgender issues remained in the shadows, with a general presumption that it was a 'mental illness'. Progress for transgender rights was slow; it was not until the new Millennium, in 2002, that the Lord Chancellor's Office published the *Government Policy Concerning Transsexual People*, which categorically challenged this assumption, stating that being transgender is a medical condition, characterised by an 'overpowering' sense of different gender identity. On 4 April 2005, the Gender Recognition Act 2004 came into force. This Act allows people to apply to receive a Gender Recognition Certificate, that shows the person has satisfied the criteria for legal recognition in a certain gender. Effectively, it allows a transgender person legal recognition as the gender with which they identify.

A year later saw the first successful prosecution for a murder aggravated by homophobic hostility. In the late hours of 14 October 2005, Jody Dobrowski was walking alone through Clapham Common. As Clapham Common was a known spot for homosexual activity, two men (Thomas Pickford and Scott Walker) saw Dobrowski and drew the conclusion that he was homosexual. They beat him to death, beating him so badly that he could only be identified by his fingerprints. Pickford and Walker pleaded guilty to Dobrowski's murder on 12 May 2006 and were sentenced to life imprisonment with a minimum term of 28 years. The Judge applied the sentencing uplift for cases marked by hostility on the grounds of sexuality, under section 146 of the Criminal Justice Act 2003.

Most recently, the Policing and Crime Act 2017 contained a section known as the 'Alan Turing law'. This officially gave posthumous pardons to the thousands of homosexual men from England and Wales who had been convicted under the old laws. Those still living were able to apply to have their convictions erased.

In July 2018, the Government announced a public Consultation about how best to reform the Gender Recognition Act 2004. In May 2019, the World Health Organisation announced that it would no longer class being transgender as a 'disorder', recognising that it is not actually a mental health condition. Nevertheless, data collected by the BBC in June 2019 suggested that the number of transgender hate crimes recorded by police forces in England, Scotland and Wales had risen by 81% as compared to the previous financial year[2].

Disability Rights

Disabled people have suffered discrimination and, indeed, persecution for thousands of years. In Ancient Greece, the cult of the 'body beautiful' saw the infanticide of disabled babies. In Ancient Rome, disabled children were drowned in the Tiber. Historically, in the United Kingdom, it is the law that has in fact enabled discrimination by keeping disabled people out of society and in institutions, making them essentially invisible.

One clear example of this stems from year 1247, and the foundation of the notorious Bethlam Royal Hospital in London, otherwise known as 'Bedlam'. Although not in fact originally created for the treatment of the mentally ill, it gradually transformed into a hospital dedicated solely to that category of society. The hospital remained entrenched as part of English society for many centuries, with 'treatments' becoming notoriously more and more tortuous.

The 16th Century is marked by mass hysteria around the phenomenon of 'witches', which resulted in the persecution of people suffering from genuine illnesses. Women who were suffering from mental illnesses could be deemed to be practicing witchcraft; so too were those women who had birthed physically disabled children, or themselves were physically disabled.

As the century drew to a close, the Poor Law Act 1597 provided the first complete code of relief for the poor, which included relief for the lame, impotent, old, blind and other poor who were unable to work.

---

2 *Transgender hate crimes recorded by police go up 81%*, 27 June 2019: https://www.bbc.co.uk/news/uk-48756370, last accessed on 28 February 2020

Moving forward to 1808, the County Asylums Act of that year established institutions – known as 'asylums' – for the poor, and for criminally insane. They were to provide specialist treatment for those suffering from mental illness. Just under forty years later, the Lunacy Act 1845 and the County Asylums Act 1845 sought to build upon the 1808 iteration. Under the Lunacy Act 1845, however, patients lost their right of access to the courts to challenge their detention; now, detention could only be reviewed by the newly established 'Commissioners in Lunacy' or county visitors.

Only twenty-one years later, the Idiots Act 1886 was passed in order to set up facilities for the care, education and training of "*idiots and imbeciles*". It set out a distinction between 'lunatics', 'idiots' and 'imbeciles' in order to differentiate between the ways in which people deemed to fall into these categories were cared for.

In 1907, the Eugenics Education Society was formed. This Society believed at that time that offering medical and social services to disabled people would lead to the degeneration of the human race. Its ideas gained prominence and support amongst influential people. Indeed, in 1911, Winston Churchill spoke in the House of Commons of the 'need' to introduce compulsory labour camps for 'mental defectives'.

The Mental Deficiency Act 1913 repealed the Idiots Act 1886. It established the Board of Control for Lunacy and Mental Deficiency to oversee provisions for the care and management of 'idiots', 'imbeciles', 'feeble-minded persons' and 'moral imbeciles'. 'Idiots' and 'imbeciles' were deemed to be incapable of managing themselves, and so might be placed in an institution or under guardianship. Therefore, those suffering from severe illnesses might find themselves removed from the eye of society, rather than allowed to integrate and to be accepted.

It was not until over thirty years later that disabled people began to receive legislative protection. In 1944, disabled people were afforded some specific employment rights, through the Disabled Persons

(Employment) Act 1944. That Act required employers with at least twenty employees to ensure that at least 3% of their workforce were disabled people.

The Mental Health Act 1959 replaced the Mental Deficiency Act 1913, with provisions aimed at integration rather than isolation. It was designed to ensure that a) generally treatment would be voluntary and informal; b) where the treatment had to be compulsory, it was governed by a legal framework and was the result of a medically informed decision; and c) treatment would be moved, where possible, away from institutional care to the community.

The Chronically Sick and Disabled Persons Act 1970 took the disabled rights' movement strides forward. It required local authorities to provide welfare services to people with certain mental or physical disabilities. The services that local authorities would need to provide under this Act included home adaptations, practical assistance in the home and help with procuring access to recreational activities.

Just over a decade later, the Mental Health Act 1983 consolidated mental health law, and (although it has been subject to various amendments) provided the system under which we operate today.

CHAPTER TWO
AN OVERVIEW OF THE LAW

This chapter is an overview of the current law in England and Wales. Later chapters will address the law in more detail. In order to understand how the different provisions inter-relate, it will be helpful to read this chapter first.

The law relating to hate crime in England and Wales cannot be found neatly presented in one spot. It is the product of years of evolution and understanding – a process that continues today, with Consultations taking place about how far its scope should extend. So it is that the current law in relation to hate crime is actually a melange of specific statutory offences, and more general provisions aimed at the sentencing stage.

It is for that reason that the discussion of the law in this chapter and, indeed, this book will be separated into two limbs: 1) statutory offences; 2) the sentencing uplift. Essentially, if the offence with which you are dealing is not a specific statutory offence, the hate crime element will be dealt with at the sentencing stage by way of the sentencing uplift provisions.

Specific Statutory Offences

There are a number of specific statutory offences that can be called 'hate crime' offences. They can be found in the following acts:

i. The Crime and Disorder Act 1998;

ii. The Public Order Act 1986;

iii. The Football Offences Act 1991;

iv. Ecclesiastical Courts Jurisdiction Act 1860;

v. The Offences Against the Person Act 1861.

The Crime and Disorder Act 1998

The offences in the Crime and Disorder Act 1998 ("the 1998 Act") are aggravated versions of the 'basic' offences. So, for example, an assault occasioning actual bodily harm under section 47 of the Offences Against the Person Act 1861 becomes an aggravated assault occasioning actual bodily harm under section 29 of the 1998 Act.

Currently, the 1998 Act only provides criminal offences that are aggravated by virtue of race or religion.

In order to prove the offence, then, the Prosecution must not only prove the basic offence but must also prove that it was racially or religiously aggravated.

Section 28 of the 1998 Act sets out the meaning of 'racially or religiously aggravated'. According to section 28(1):

> "*An offence is racially or religiously aggravated for the purposes of sections 29 to 32 below if—*
>
> *(a) at the time of committing the offence, or immediately before or after doing so, the offender demonstrates towards the victim of the offence hostility based on the victim's membership (or presumed membership) of a racial or religious group; or*
>
> *(b) the offence is motivated (wholly or partly) by hostility towards members of a racial or religious group based on their membership of that group.*"

Although this section expressly limits its definition of 'racially or religiously aggravated' to the specific offences set out in the 1998 Act, we shall see this wording mirrored in other legislation dealing with hate crime offences.

So we can see that whether an offence is racially or religiously motivated depends upon whether one of two conditions are satisfied:

i. Whether the offender *demonstrates* hostility towards the victim based on their membership or presumed membership of a racial or religious group, *at the time of committing the offence or immediately before or after doing so*;

ii. The offence can be said to be *motivated* (either wholly or in part) by hostility towards members of a racial or religious group based on their membership of that group.

Demonstrating hostility may be relatively easier to prove: very often, it might take the form of words spoken at the time of the attack. Proving motivation, however, requires delving into the mind of the defendant – a notoriously difficult thing to do. Examples of actions that might prove motivation, however, could be a history of committing crimes against members of a certain group, or telephone messages sent on a previous occasion that indicate their hostility towards a certain group. This will be considered in more detail in Chapter 4.

Sections 28(2) to (3) clarify that 'membership' includes association with members of that group, 'presumed' means presumed by the offender and that it is immaterial whether the hostility is also based on a factor other than race or religion.

Section 28(4) states that 'racial group' means a group of persons defined by reference to race, colour, nationality (including citizenship) or ethnic or national origins. Section 28(5) states that 'religious group' means a group of persons defined by reference to religious belief or lack of religious belief.

We can see, then, that racially aggravated offences are not confined simply to those victims who might be of a separate race to the offender, but also applies to those victims who are targeted due to their citizenship, their national origins, ethnicity or colour.

Additionally, religiously aggravated offences do not simply apply to those victims who hold a religious belief and are so targeted; under this definition, an atheist or agnostic might just as easily be able to avail themselves of the protection of the 1998 Act.

We will analyse key definitions further in Chapter 3.

For now, though, having been introduced to section 28 of the 1998 Act, we move onto the specific statutory offences. These are set out in sections 29 to 32 of the 1998 Act.

Section 29 addresses racially and religiously aggravated assaults. Section 29(1)(a) applies to offences committed under section 20 of the Offences Against the Person Act 1861 (malicious wounding / grievous bodily harm). Section 29(1)(b) covers offences under section 47 of the same Act (assault occasioning actual bodily harm). Section 29(1)(c) covers the offence of common assault. Section 29 provides that a person commits an offence under that section if he commits one of those three assaults, and that assault is racially or religiously aggravated.

All three assaults then attract greater sentences than their counterparts. In addition, all three are 'either way' offences (i.e. can be heard in the Crown Court or the Magistrates' Court). By comparison, the basic version of common assault can only be heard in the Magistrates' Court.

Section 30 of the 1998 Act creates an offence of racially or religiously aggravated criminal damage. Again, the section provides that a person is guilty of an offence if they commit the basic act of criminal damage under the Criminal Damage Act 1971, and that offence is racially or religiously aggravated for the purposes of the section. The defendant convicted of this offence is liable to a greater sentence than under the basic offence – on conviction on Indictment, he can be imprisoned for a term not exceeding fourteen years, or a fine, or both. Compare this to the basic offence, for which the maximum penalty is ten years' imprisonment.

Section 31 sets out three racially or religiously aggravated public order offences. In a similar vein to the sections that preceded it, it provides that a person is guilty of an offence if he commits an offence under: (i) section 4 of the Public Order Act 1986 (fear or provocation of violence); (ii) section 4A of the same Act (intentional harassment, alarm or distress); (iii) section 5 of the same Act (harassment, alarm or distress) – and it is racially or religiously aggravated. Once more, the sentences are increased for the aggravated versions of the offences.

Section 31(6) of the 1998 Act specifically provides that, on trial on Indictment for the aggravated versions of section 4 or section 4A of the Public Order Act 1986, the jury may acquit the defendant of the aggravated offence and find him guilty of the basic offence.

Finally, section 32 of the 1998 Act deals with racially or religiously aggravated harassment. This section provides that a person is guilty of an offence if he commits (i) an offence under section 2 of the Protection from Harassment Act 1997 (harassment and stalking); (ii) an offence under section 4 of that same Act (putting people in fear of violence and stalking involving fear of violence or serious alarm or distress) – and it is racially or religiously aggravated. Again, the sentences are increased.

As in section 31, section 32(6) explicitly provides that the jury may acquit the defendant of the aggravated offences and convict him of a basic offence mentioned in the section.

Public Order Act 1986

For our purposes, the key part of the Public Order Act 1986 ("the 1986 Act") is Part III. This Part sets out offences falling under the banner headline: 'Incitement to Racial Hatred'.

Section 17 of the 1986 Act defines racial hatred:

> *"In this Part "racial hatred" means hatred against a group of persons defined by reference to colour, race, nationality (including citizenship) or ethnic or national origins."*

The wording is, as we can see, the same as in section 28 of the 1998 Act above.

The 1986 Act relates to the following broad actions:

i. Use of words or behaviour;

ii. The display of written material;

iii. Public performance of a play;

iv. Distributing, showing or playing a recording;

v. Broadcasting or including a programme in a cable programme service;

vi. Possession of inflammatory material.

The 1998 Act makes it an offence to carry out any of these actions if, in doing so, (i) the person intends to stir up hatred on the basis of race, religion or sexual orientation; or (ii) having regard to all the circumstances, hatred on either of those three bases is likely to be stirred up.

Section 18 of the Act provides that it is an offence to use threatening, abusive or insulting words or behaviour, or to display any written material that is threatening, abusive or insulting if (i) the person intends to stir up racial hatred; or (ii) racial hatred is likely to be stirred up.

However, the accused has a statutory defence (under section 18(4) of the 1998 Act) if he can prove that he was inside a dwelling and had no reason to believe that the words, or written material, would be heard or seen by a person outside that or any other dwelling. So it is that the accused is protected from words said within his or another person's home, provided that he had no reason to believe that the words would spread any further.

Section 29B of the 1998 Act mirrors section 18, aside from the fact that it applies to religious hatred or hatred on the grounds of sexual orientation.

Section 19 of the 1998 Act provides that a person who publishes or distributes material which is threatening, abusive or insulting is guilty of an offence if (i) he intends to stir up racial hatred; or (ii) having regard to all the circumstances, racial hatred is likely to be stirred up thereby. It therefore follows extremely similar lines as section 18 of the same Act.

The accused has a statutory defence to this offence under section 19(2) of the 1998 Act, if he proves that he was not aware of the content of the material and did not suspect, nor had reason to suspect, that it was threatening, abusive or insulting.

Section 29C mirrors section 19 of the same Act, aside from that it applies to religious hatred or hatred on the grounds of sexual orientation.

Section 20 of the 1998 Act provides that any person who presents or directs the performance of a play that involves threatening, abusive or insulting words or behaviour is guilty of an offence if he intends to stir up racial hatred or, having regard to all the circumstances (and, in particular, taking the performance as a whole) racial hatred is likely to be stirred up thereby.

Section 20(2) provides a statutory defence if the person is not shown to have intended to stir up racial hatred. In that case, it is a defence for the accused to prove that he did not know, and had no reason to suspect, that the performance would involve the use of offending words or behaviour; or that he did not know, and had no reason to suspect, that the offending words or behaviour were threatening, abusive or insulting; or that he did not know and had no reason to suspect that the circumstances in which the performance would be given would be such that racial hatred would be likely to be stirred up.

Section 20(3) of the 1998 Act provides some exceptions to the application of the section, such as where a performance is given solely or primarily for purpose of a rehearsal.

Section 29D mimics the offence in section 20, aside from that it applies to religious hatred or hatred on the grounds of sexual orientation.

Section 21 of the 1998 Act creates an offence of distributing, showing or playing a recording of images or sounds that are threatening, abusive or insulting if (i) the person intends thereby to stir up racial hatred; (ii) racial hatred is likely to be stirred up thereby.

There is a statutory defence under section 21(3) if the accused can show that he was not aware of the content of the recording and did not suspect, nor had reason to suspect, that it was threatening, abusive or insulting.

Section 29E mimics this offence, aside from that it applies to religious hatred and hatred on the grounds of sexual orientation.

Section 22 creates an offence of broadcasting or including a programme in a cable programme service involving threatening, abusive or insulting visual images or sounds if (i) he intends thereby to stir up racial hatred; or (ii) having regard to all the circumstances, racial hatred is likely to be stirred up thereby.

Much as with the other offences in this Act, there are statutory defences available should the accused prove that he did not have knowledge, or suspicion, of the inclusion of the programme or the use of offending material.

Section 29F creates the same offence applicable to religious hatred and to hatred on the grounds of sexual orientation.

Finally, section 23 covers the possession of racially inflammatory material – it makes it an offence to possess written material, or recording of visual images or sounds, which are threatening, abusive or insulting, with a view to – essentially – showing or distributing the material, if he (i) intends to stir up racial hatred; or (ii) racial hatred is likely to be stirred up thereby.

There is a statutory defence under section 23(3) where the accused proves that he was not aware of the content of the written material or recording and did not suspect, nor had reason to suspect, that it was threatening, abusive or insulting.

Section 29G creates the same offence in respect of religious hatred or hatred on the grounds of sexual orientation.

<u>Football Offences Act 1991</u>

The Football Offences Act 1991 ("the 1991 Act") creates the following offence at section 3:

> "***3. Indecent or racialist chanting.***
>
> *(1) It is an offence to engage or take part in chanting of an indecent or racialist nature at a designated football match.*

(2) For this purpose—

(a) "chanting" means the repeated uttering of any words or sounds (whether alone or in concert with one more others); and

(b) "of a racialist nature" means consisting of or including matter which is threatening, abusive or insulting to a person by reason of his colour, race, nationality (including citizenship) or ethnic or national origins."

We can see that, once more, the definition of 'race' encompasses colour, race, nationality (including citizenship) or ethnic or national origins. It is also clear that there is no requirement that the chanting be directed at a particular person or group present at the football match; it is enough to prove that the racialist words or sounds were chanted at the football match.

The Ecclesiastical Courts Jurisdiction Act 1860

Section 2 of the Ecclesiastical Courts Jurisdiction Act 1860 creates an offence of violent or indecent behaviour in any place of worship that is certified under the Places of Worship Registration Act 1855; this includes mosques and synagogues. The Act also affords those people preaching, or carrying out other religious duties, protection.

Offences Against the Person Act 1861

Section 36 of the Offences Against the Person Act 1861 makes it an offence to use threats or force in order to obstruct or prevent, or try to obstruct or prevent, a clergyman or other minister from officiating in – essentially – their official duties within the church, chapel, meeting house or 'other place of divine worship'.

Sentencing Uplift

This brings us to those offences that are not provided for in the legislation above, but have nevertheless involved hostility based on race, religion, sexual orientation, gender identity or disability.

It is interesting to note that the statutory offences only address race, religion and sexual orientation (and, in fact, sexual orientation is only provided for in the Public Order Act 1998). There are, then, potentially a number of instances where a crime involving hostility on one of these grounds will have been committed for which there is no specific statutory offence.

Sections 145 and 146 of the Criminal Justice Act 2003 ("the 2003 Act") provide a broad brush approach to all such offences.

Section 145 of the Criminal Justice Act 2003

Sections 145 of the 2003 Act states:

> "***145. Increase in sentences for racial or religious aggravation***
>
> *(1) This section applies where a court is considering the seriousness of an offence other than one under sections 29 to 32 of the Crime and Disorder Act 1998 (c. 37) (racially or religiously aggravated assaults, criminal damage, public order offences and harassment etc).*
>
> *(2) If the offence was racially or religiously aggravated, the court—*
>
> > *(a) must treat that fact as an aggravating factor, and*
> >
> > *(b) must state in open court that the offence was so aggravated.*
>
> *(3) Section 28 of the Crime and Disorder Act 1998 (meaning of "racially or religiously aggravated") applies for the purposes of this section as it applies for the purposes of sections 29 to 32 of that Act.*"

This section therefore:

i. Expressly applies only to those offences that are racially or religiously aggravated;

ii. Explicitly excludes those provided for by sections 29 to 32 of the 1998 Act, set out above;

iii. Adopts the meaning of 'racially or religiously aggravated' under section 28 of the 1998 Act.

Section 146 of the Criminal Justice Act 2003

Section 146 of the 2003 Act deals with hostility on the basis of disability, sexual orientation and transgender identity:

> "***146. Increase in sentences for aggravation related to disability, sexual orientation or transgender identity***
>
> *(1) This section applies where the court is considering the seriousness of an offence committed in any of the circumstances mentioned in subsection (2).*
>
> *(2) Those circumstances are—*
>
> *(a) that, at the time of committing the offence, or immediately before or after doing so, the offender demonstrated towards the victim of the offence hostility based on—*
>
> *(i) the sexual orientation (or presumed sexual orientation) of the victim,*
>
> *(ii) a disability (or presumed disability) of the victim, or*
>
> *(iii) the victim being (or being presumed to be) transgender, or*
>
> *(b) that the offence is motivated (wholly or partly)—*

(i) by hostility towards persons who are of a particular sexual orientation,

(ii) by hostility towards persons who have a disability or a particular disability, or

(iii) by hostility towards persons who are transgender.

(3) The court—

(a) must treat the fact that the offence was committed in any of those circumstances as an aggravating factor, and

(b) must state in open court that the offence was committed in such circumstances.

(4) It is immaterial for the purposes of paragraph (a) or (b) of subsection (2) whether or not the offender's hostility is also based, to any extent, on any other factor not mentioned in that paragraph.

(5) In this section "disability" means any physical or mental impairment.

(6) In this section references to being transgender include references to being transsexual, or undergoing, proposing to undergo or having undergone a process or part of a process of gender reassignment."

This section therefore:

i. Expressly applies only to hostility based on sexual orientation, transgender identity or disability;

ii. Expressly states that it is immaterial whether or not the hostility is also based – to any extent – on any other factor;

iii. Defines 'disability' as physical or mental impairment;

iv. Clarifies that references to being transgender include references to being transsexual or undergoing, proposing to undergo or having undergone a process – or part of a process – of gender reassignment.

These two sections of the 2003 Act ensure that all offences that involve a hate crime element are subject to an uplift in the sentence imposed, even where they are not specific hate crime offences in and of themselves.

Sentencing Hate Crimes: The Staged Approach

When sentencing a hate crime offence, the Court should follow a 'staged' approach – first, consider what the sentence would have been without the element of aggravation, and then consider what the sentence should be with the element of aggravation. This follows the guidance of the Court of Appeal in *Kelly and Donnelly* [2001] EWCA Crim 170; at paragraph 62:

> "*... a sentencer should first arrive at the appropriate sentence, without the element of racial aggravation but including any other aggravating or mitigating factors. The sentence should then be enhanced to take account of the racial aggravation ...*"

Although the Court in that case was concerned with a racially aggravated offence, there would seem to be no reason why that should not extend to all hate crime offences. This guidance was affirmed in *Higgins* (2009) EWCA Crim 708.

Note that sections 145 and 146 of the 2003 Act also require the Judge, once he or she has determined that an offence falls under those provisions and is therefore aggravated, to announce that the offence is so aggravated. There is no similar requirement in the provisions of the particular statutory offences. This makes sense – after all, the aggravation is made explicit in the title of the offence, and there is no need to require the Judge to reiterate that point.

The Judge should, therefore, be invited to:

i. State that the offence is aggravated by virtue of falling under sections 145 or 146 of the 2003 Act (if applicable);

ii. Announce what the sentence would have been without the hate crime element;

iii. Announce what the sentence is, having been aggravated to take account of the hate crime element.

CHAPTER THREE
KEY CONCEPTS IN THE LAW OF HATE CRIME

This chapter discusses the key words and concepts that you will come across when working on a hate crime case. The words and concepts discussed in this chapter are ones that span across all the various sections of the legislation relating to hate crime, and so this chapter will help you in applying any aspect of the criminal law in relation to hate. Words and concepts that are specific only to a certain section of legislation are discussed in the chapters about those sections.

We have seen in Chapter Two that, although much else may differ amongst the various strands of legislation, there are three key concepts that repeat themselves time and again. They are the core elements of many hate crimes, and are as follows:

i. Hostility;

ii. A person demonstrating hostility.

iii. A person being motivated by hostility;

In addition, this chapter will consider the meaning of 'race', 'religion', 'sexual orientation', 'disability' and 'transgender identity' – the scope of application of those concepts in the law does not always reflect the way in which we use those words in everyday life.

Hostility

There is no precise, legal definition of hostility. In the absence of any such definition, we should use its ordinary, everyday meaning.

For our assistance as to what that ordinary, everyday meaning looks like, we can turn to the Oxford English Dictionary. This defines hostility as: "*aggressive or unfriendly feelings or behaviour*".

Therefore, neither violence nor, in fact, aggression are needed for hostility to exist. We need only be sure that there is negative – or 'unfriendly' – feeling.

Demonstrating Hostility

One way in which a hate crime can be proven is to show that the accused was demonstrating hostility based on the protected characteristic (or the presumed protected characteristic) of the victim at the time of – or immediately before or after – committing the offence.

What constitutes a demonstration?

Implicit in the word 'demonstrate' is the existence of word or action that make the meaning behind them clear. For example, shouting a racial slur is a clear demonstration of hostility on the grounds of race.

However, the offender need not have resorted to well-known racial slurs in order to demonstrate hostility. Words that may be 'innocent' in other contexts can become hostile when said in a certain way, in certain environments, or with the addition of swear words. So, for example, most people could agree that the word 'African' itself is not a slur. However, when teamed with a swear word so that it becomes 'African bitch', it becomes a clear demonstration of hostility (as in the case of *White* [2001] EWCA Crim 216). Similarly, 'black' is not in itself generally considered to be a slur; the phrase 'black bastard', though, is another matter (as in *Woods* [2002] EWHC 85).

Hostile phrases need not be spoken to be demonstrated. Hostility could be demonstrated by the wearing of a swastika, or singing certain songs (see the comments of the House of Lords in *Rogers* [2007] UKHL 8). It could also be demonstrated by, for example, holding up a banner with offensive language displayed on it (*G & T v DPP* [2004] EWHC 183).

Demonstration versus Motivation

As we have seen, the Crime and Disorder Act 1998 and the uplift provisions in the Criminal Justice Act 2003 provide two possible routes to proving the requisite hostility: a) the offender demonstrates hostility at the time of the offence, or immediately before or after; or b) the offender is motivated by hostility. If either limb is satisfied, that is enough; there is no need to prove the other.

It follows that once the demonstration of hostility can be proven, there is no need to delve into why they demonstrated that hostility, to consider the underlying motivation or whether they have a history of prejudicial belief. In other words, uttering the words, displaying the banner or wearing the swastika is enough.

By way of example, in *DPP v McFarlane* [2002] EWHC 485, the defendant yelled racial abuse at the victim, who had parked in a disabled bay. The defendant had been entitled to park there, and so arguably was rather strongly (perhaps primarily) motivated by his sense of injustice at his parking spot having been taken, rather than due to a desire to express deep seated racist views. However, his motivation was immaterial to whether the offence was proven. He demonstrated hostility based on race at the time of the offence, and so the hate crime element was complete.

In the same vein, the High Court in *Woods* (*supra*), rejected the defence contention that the defendant had been in such a frustrated frame of mind when he called the victim a 'black bastard' that he would have reached for any insult applicable to the person in front of him – i.e. it just so happened that the victim was black and so the defendant used that to insult him, rather than that the defendant held deep seated racist views. At paragraph 13:

> "*Thirdly, it is submitted [by the prosecution] that the fact that the respondent's frame of mind was such that he would have abused any person standing in the complainant's shoes by reference to an obvious physical character is irrelevant. In my judgment, this submission is well-founded. If the respondent would have assaulted another person and called him, say, "a fat bastard", that would not be an aggravated offence because Parliament has not found it necessary to provide additional protection to the overweight by the creation of an aggravated form of the offence by reference to that characteristic. Racial abuse, however, is the subject of an aggravated offence, and therefore the evidence in this case fell to be considered by reference to that category rather than to circumstances which would have obtained if the abuse had referred to characteristics which have not received the attention of Parliament.*"

It is clear, then, that once the hostility based on a protected characteristic is demonstrated, that part of the offence is complete, regardless of motivation.

When we consider the societal mischief that the law is addressing, we can see the reasoning behind this approach. As we have seen in Chapter One, the history behind demonstrations of prejudicial hostility is a complex and raw one. Prejudicial words have been used to ostracise, to demean and to mock people from certain groups for centuries. Even where there might be little genuine belief behind the words – and the defendant might swear with feeling that he is not a racist or a homophobe, because his circle of dearest friends includes people of all skin tones and sexual orientation – the easy resort to words with such a dark history cannot be tolerated. When it comes to hostile words based on membership of a long-oppressed group, we cannot assume that the old children's rhyme is true: "*sticks and stones may break my bones, but words can never hurt me*". Sometimes the prejudicial words may burn a lot deeper, and for far longer, than the sting of the physical blow.

The Immediacy Requirement

It is a requirement in the law that the demonstration must take place either at the time of committing the basic offence, or *immediately* before or after doing so. The question then arises: when does something cease to be 'immediately' before or after the offence? Must the demonstration be within a matter of seconds, minutes, tens of minutes or more?

The High Court in Parry v DPP [2004] EWHC 3112 (Admin) held that the hostile act had to occur in the 'immediate context of the substantive offence'. In that case, the appellant had thrown nail varnish on his neighbour's door (as later admitted by him in interview). Some twenty minutes after he had thrown the nail varnish, the police spoke to the appellant who stated: "*those Irish cunts have been stealing my son's trainers ...*" and when warned about his language, "*I can say what I like about those IRA bastards in my own home*". The argument on appeal was that the lower courts had erred in finding that the words were uttered immediately after the event. In accepting this submission, the High Court stated at paragraph 21:

> "*No Crown Court properly directing itself as to the meaning and effect of section 28(1) could reasonably have made this finding. The statement was not made in the immediate context of the substantive offence, but was made by the appellant after he had quit the scene and was sitting in his own house, at least 20 minutes after the door had been damaged.*"

The Court of Appeal resurrected the question of immediacy in Babbs (Richard John) [2007] EWCA Crim 2737. The appellant had been convicted of racially aggravated assault by beating. The facts of the offence were as follows: the victim and his companion were waiting in a queue at a restaurant. The appellant was also in the queue, and affected by drink. The appellant started to abuse the victim and his companion; during the course of this, the appellant said: "*You're living on the system. You're conning the system. You foreign fuckers, you do not deserve to be here*". There was a scuffle, which staff managed to quell. For a time, between five and fifteen minutes, all was relatively calm. However, there came a time when the appellant 'jumped the queue' and reached the front before the victim. The appellant waved his bag of food in front of the victim, upon which the victim was said (by the appellant) to have called the appellant 'white trash'. The appellant then headbutted the victim. It was the headbutt upon which the charge was based.

On appeal, it was argued on behalf of the appellant that there was no connection between the racially charged words used by the appellant and the assault sufficient to meet the immediacy requirements of the Act. In rejecting this submission, the Court of Appeal stated at paragraph 8 of their Judgment:

> "*It seems to us that the judge was entitled to leave the matter to the jury. Although he talked in terms of continuum, the point that is of importance in the subsection is that it is directed not so much to words but to the hostility which is demonstrated towards a victim with the relevant connotation. The words used by the appellant were, it seems to us, capable of colouring the behaviour of the appellant throughout the subsequent events. He had evinced hostility which, by reason of the words he used, could be said to have been based upon race. The jury were perfectly entitled to conclude that the hostility shown later was based upon the same reasoning, if reasoning is the right description of it, that had been evinced in the words that the appellant had used earlier and, accordingly, that hostility based upon race was evinced over a continuing period from the moment that the words were first used to the moment that it exploded into the ultimate violence in question.*"

The key point, then, is not that a delay of fifteen minutes is sufficient to be 'immediate' and a delay of twenty minutes is not, but rather to consider the context of each case. In the former case, the substantive offence was completed and the defendant had left the scene; he uttered the relevant words to a police officer away from the scene of the crime when in his own home, rather than at some point during the hostile environment surrounding the offence. In the latter case, the jury were entitled to find that racial hostility was in fact being continually demonstrated by the defendant from the time of the words spoken right through to the headbutt, and so it was a continuing racially hostile environment, albeit that he did not utter the words again right before he assaulted the victim.

The victim need not hear or see the hostile words used, though. In Parry v DPP (*supra*), the High Court held that hostility could be demonstrated even if the victim was absent, so long as the hostility had occurred in the immediate context of the substantive offence.

Relevance of the Victim's Perception

An apparent lack of impact upon the victim is not generally relevant to the question of whether hostility has in fact been demonstrated. In Woods (*supra*), the doorman to a club refused entry to the defendant's friend. The defendant assaulted the doorman, immediately beforehand calling him a "*black bastard*". The victim had given evidence at the Magistrates' Court, saying that he was "*not bothered*" by racial language used, "*so long as they don't touch me...*". The Magistrates found that the defendant had uttered the words 'black bastard' but, in acquitting the defendant of the racially aggravated offence, stated:

> "*We took into account how the victim assaulted perceived the comments. In his evidence [the doorman] made no play (at any stage) of the words being racially offensive and said he was not bothered by such comments ...*"

In allowing the Prosecutor's Appeal by way of Case Stated, the High Court stated (at paragraph 10 of their Judgment):

> *"In the course of his submissions, [the Prosecution] has taken a number of points. First, he submits that the Justices were wrong to take into account the victim's perception of the words. I agree with this submission. The fact that the person to whom the words were directed may have had a personality which enables him to take a resilient or broad shouldered view of the situation is irrelevant to the question which arises under section 28(1)(a), namely whether the offender "demonstrates towards the victim ... hostility based on the victim's membership of a racial group"."*

This decision must, in my submission, be correct. There may be numerous reasons why a person may state they are 'not bothered' by prejudicial abuse. They may not wish to be seen as a 'victim' or 'causing a fuss', they may fear repercussions within their community or they may be so used to hearing prejudicial abuse that it is normalised in their minds, for example. By way of analogy, if a person is violently beaten by their abuser and claims it is not so bad, because they have normalised such assaults from their abuser or fear repercussions, we do not simply close our eyes to the very real fact that an assault has taken place. In the same vein, the hate crime complainant's resilience to, or normalisation of, the hostility demonstrated against them should not colour the tribunal's decision as to whether hostility has in fact been demonstrated.

Group Offending and the Demonstration of Hostility

The case may arise where there are multiple offenders taking part in an offence. A simple example may be an assault, where a group of people attack another. During that attack, imagine that one person yells racial abuse.

It is an established principle of criminal law that where multiple offenders take part in an offence, they are all deemed to be guilty of that offence, even where their roles are different. So the person who holds a man down so that others may steal from his pockets is just as guilty of robbery as the people doing the stealing. In our example of a person yelling racial abuse during a group attack, does the principle of joint enterprise make all within the group guilty of a hate crime?

In *R v Davies and Ely* [2003] EWCA Crim 3700, the defendants were convicted of causing grievous bodily harm under section 18 of the Offences Against the Person Act 1861. The facts were that Davies had been the victim of a burglary, and believed that his ex-partner (Becky Taylor) knew who had committed the offence. Davies and a group of companions had been drinking and set off to find Ms Taylor. Davies and Ely were both armed. They found Ms Taylor with the eventual victim, Mr Carter. There was an argument. Mr Carter was punched and fell to the floor. In the ensuing attack, Carter was stabbed in the back. An independent witness heard a member of the group say "*You black bastard, I am going to cut you*".

When sentencing, the Judge found that there was no element of racial motivation when the group initially set off. He did find, however, that racial aggravation "*came from your group at a time when this victim was subject to or shortly before he was subject to an attack*". The Judge therefore applied a sentencing uplift. It was that aspect of the sentence that was appealed by the defendants.

In allowing the appeal, the Court of Appeal noted that the Judge made no finding as to who said the racially charged words; the Court added that it could not do so either. At paragraph 8:

> "*Though it was open to all members of this group to be convicted of a section 18 offence on a joint enterprise basis, in our judgment that same basis is not apt to make all members of the group criminally liable for the added aggravating feature of racial aggravation, as was the case in the judgment of the judge here. This is not a conclusion we feel able to embrace with great enthusiasm. Clearly somebody in that group said these words and had those feelings of hostility in his mind. But in our judgment the words of the statute are plain ...in view of the findings that the learned judge made, and particularly his inab-*

> *ility to find from whose mouth this offending remark came and specifically that it came from one or other of these appellants, we are driven to allow these appeals...*"

The wording of the legislation clearly states that the offender must have demonstrated hostility; those words cannot therefore be interpreted to extend to others within a group who may not have individually demonstrated that hostility. As in the case of Davies and Ely, where the demonstration cannot be attributed to a particular person within a group, none should be sentenced on the aggravated basis.

Notwithstanding this decision, hostility may be demonstrated by joining, and showing adherence to, a group that itself demonstrates racial hostility. In the case of G and T v DPP (*supra*), the defendants were charged with racially aggravated offences relating to their harassment of a Somalian family, as part of a group of youths. The District Judge had found that a notable feature of the group included the consistent racially abusive reference to Somalians, usually in the form of words or gestures, including monkey noises. The offences culminated in an affray involving the group and a member of the targeted family. The two defendants had been part of that affray and assaulted the victim by kicking.

The District Judge convicted the defendants of the offences charged. She stated that, given her findings, she was entitled to find that the affray had features of racial aggravation, which would be taken into account when sentencing. The matter was appealed by way of Case Stated asking, amongst other things, whether the District Judge had been correct to find that racial hostility was demonstrated through consistent membership of a group that carried out racially motivated actions.

At paragraph 13 of its decision, the High Court decided:

> *"It is, in my judgment, evident from the wording of that section that section 28(1)(a) requires the prosecution to prove facts which indicate that the offender had demonstrated racial hostility at the time of committing the offence or immediately before or after doing so. That is not so much to indicate the offender's state of mind as to prove what he did or said so as to demonstrate racial hostility towards the victim. Often the demonstration will be by words or shouting. It may equally be possible to demonstrate racial hostility by means of doing something other than literally by means of words, as, for instance, by holding up a banner with racially offensive language on it. Equally, in my judgment, an offender may demonstrate racial hostility by joining in the activities of a group of people where a sufficient number of members of the group are themselves demonstrating racial hostility, and where the defendant's adherence to the group is such as to go beyond mere presence within the group, but so as to associate himself or herself with the demonstration of racial hostility which the group as a whole is displaying."*

So it is we see that there is a clear distinction draw between a) being part of a group committing an offence, where one or more members happen to demonstrate the requisite hostility; and b) being part of a group who has as a very characteristic the demonstration of the requisite hostility. In the latter case, the offender, in choosing to be part of such a group, can be said to be demonstrating the requisite hostility himself.

Motivated by Hostility

Whilst the 'demonstration of hostility' limb is concerned simply with what the offender did, the 'motivation' limb is concerned with why the offender acted in that way. It is one of the few instances of criminal law where the Prosecution must prove the purpose of the offender's actions rather than simply their intent to do something, and the fact that they did that.

It stands to reason that proving 'motivation' may often be more difficult than proving that the offender demonstrated hostility. A racially offensive banner, or a homophobic slur, are unambiguous demonstrations of hostility. We need not rely on supposition, or inference. By contrast, proving motivation will, with few exceptions, rely on us piecing together various nuggets of evidence in order to draw an inference as to the workings of the offender's mind.

Motivated Wholly or In Part

Section 28(1)(b) of the 1998 Act states:

> "*(b) the offence is motivated (wholly or partly) by hostility towards members of a racial or religious group based on their membership of that group*".

Similarly, section 146 of the 2003 Act states, in relation to hate crimes based on sexual orientation, disability or transgender identity:

> "*(b) that the offence is motivated (wholly or partly)—*
>
> > *(i) by hostility towards persons who are of a particular sexual orientation,*
> >
> > *(ii) by hostility towards persons who have a disability or a particular disability, or*
> >
> > *(iii) by hostility towards persons who are transgender.*"

It is clear from the wording of the legislation, then, that the motive for the crime need not be wholly – or even primarily – hostility against a protected characteristic. It is enough to prove that at least part of the offender's motivation was that hostility.

In certain cases, this may be demonstrable by reference to the lack of any other obvious motivation. For example, a random assault committed against a member of the LGBTQ community may lack any other obvious motivation, when we learn that the offender has a history of assaults against members of that community.

In many other cases, however, there may be numerous motives that could (or, indeed, are) underlie the action. For example, a robbery committed by a group of white youths against a black person may have acquisition of money as its primary motivation. When we learn that the white youths are members of a gang known for racial abuse against black members of the community, it may be that racial hostility is another possible motivation.

Evidence that May Prove Motivation

What sort of evidence might the Prosecution rely upon to prove that the offender was motivated by hostility due to a protected characteristic? There is no exhaustive list, and relatively little guidance. Essentially, the evidence will be that which gives insight into the workings of the offender's brain, and the factors that drive him or her.

Examples, then, could be: a) social media postings; b) possession of insignia; c) possession of inflammatory material; d) membership of certain groups (such as far right groups); e) previous incidents, or offences, targeting similar victims (e.g. a string of previous attacks against a member of the travelling community, where the current offence is also targeted at a member of the travelling community); f) diary entries or letters; g) evidence from close associates, friends or family as to words spoken in the past, or attitudes demonstrated.

Targeted versus Motivated By

There is an important distinction to draw between offences that target members of a certain community because, for example, they are perceived to be 'an easy target' – and offences that are motivated by hostility against that community. The latter would be a hate crime, attracting the legislative protections and the announcement that it is a hate crime in open court. The former would not – although the deliberate targeting of a vulnerable victim would undoubtedly constitute an aggravating factor when it came to sentencing (and so, in practical terms, the sentence either way may not be too different).

We may take a hypothetical example to illustrate this point. A young man with numerous physical and mental difficulties (who we shall call 'A') is befriended by two other young men ('B' and 'C') at a local community centre. B and C spend time getting to know A, and A trusts them. A usually takes a taxi home, with cash given to him by his parents. One evening, however, B and C offer to walk A home – a journey that lasts no longer than fifteen minutes but involves cutting through a dark stretch of pathway. A agrees. When the trio reach the pathway, B and C turn on A, punching him to the floor and kicking him. They then rob him and run away. No slurs are spoken during the incident, and B and C have no social media postings, writings or other evidence to indicate that they harbour particular animosity towards disabled people. However, both do have previous convictions for robbery and thefts from shops, with the victims coming from various strata of society. As it happens, both B and C are identified because another member of the community centre saw them leave with A. When arrested and interviewed, both admit to the crime. When asked why they chose to rob A, they said that they knew his parents often gave him a good amount of cash for the evening, to ensure that he could get a taxi home. They both said that they thought A would be an easy target, and they knew they could easily both gain his trust and overpower him. When pushed further, they admitted that they knew, through their interactions with A, that A would be unlikely to describe in great detail what has happened and they counted on A being unable to effectively identify them.

In that above example, the Prosecution can certainly prove that B and C targeted A due to his disability. They perceived A to be an 'easy target', and an unreliable witness. They knew that they could gain A's trust, and overpower him with relative ease.

However, it would be difficult for the Prosecution to prove that B and C were motivated by hostility against A because he was disabled. They have no history of attacking disabled people. They have no social media posts mocking disabled people, no diary entries or no witnesses who can say that B and C have ever displayed animosity towards disabled people. No prejudical words were spoken at the scene (and, of course, had they been, the Prosecution could have satisfied the 'demonstrated' limb in any event). Their sole motivation appears to have been acquisition of money. This is further supported by the fact that they are habitual robbers – choosing their victims on the sole criteria of who might be an easy target. In that way, they might as easily have applied the same logic to a pregnant woman, or an elderly person.

Our hypothetical scenario illustrates the fine line between a crime that is motivated by hostility towards a certain section of society, and a crime that targets a member of that section of society due to a weakness (or perceived weakness) on the part of the victim. The latter takes advantage of a person's innate characteristic – the former expresses hatred against that person for their innate characteristic. Both are, arguably, as morally repugnant as the other. However, the legislation relating to hate crime currently addresses feelings of hatred, and the expression of those feelings through criminal acts. Targeting a person based on assumptions about their level of vulnerability to your attack is not, without more, an expression of hatred for the purposes of being a hate crime. As noted above, though, it is usually an aggravating feature in sentencing guidance.

Protected Groups

What Constitutes a Racial or Religious Group?

At first blush, the answer to the question 'what is a racial or religious group' may seem to be a simple one. 'Race' and 'religion' are concepts that we use in our everyday lives. However, as with much else in the law, the lines are never straightforward. For example, does identifying someone as an 'immigrant' reach the threshold of defining them by racial group? If a Jewish person is targeted for being Jewish, is he being targeted because of his membership of a religious group, racial group – or both?

A good starting point for questions such as these is almost always the legislation. The Crime and Disorder Act addresses the meaning of racial and religious groups at, first, section 28(4), in relation to racial group:

> "*(4) In this section "racial group" means a group of persons defined by reference to race, colour, nationality (including citizenship) or ethnic or national origins.*"

And then at section 28(5), in relation to religious group:

> "*(5) In this section "religious group" means a group of persons defined by reference to religious belief or lack of religious belief.*"

As we have seen in the 'legal overview' section, this definition applies not only to crimes under section 29 of the 1998 Act, but also the statutory uplift under section 145 of the 2003 Act.

Section 17 of the Public Order Act 1986 addresses racial grouping only, providing a definition in much the same terms:

> "*In this Part "racial hatred" means hatred against a group of persons defined by reference to colour, race, nationality (including citizenship) or ethnic or national origins.*"

Finally, section 3 of the Football Offences Act 1991 creates an offence of racialist chanting at a football match. It provides that 'racialist' means material that is threatening, abusive or insulting "*...by reason of his colour, race, nationality (including citizenship) or ethnic or national origins.*"

We can see that the common thread in the legislation is that the meaning of 'racial group' is wider than that which we might use in everyday speak – it encompasses not only the person's race, but also his colour, nationality, citizenship, ethnic and national origins.

Similarly, 'religious group', as defined in section 28 of the 1998 Act, does not simply refer to a person's religious beliefs, as we might use it in everyday language. It is broad enough to include lack of religious belief – so protecting those who do not identify with a particular religion at all.

The wide scope of the term 'racial group' has been affirmed by the courts. In *Rogers* (2007) UKHL 8, the appellant had been convicted of using racially aggravated abusive or insulting words or behaviour with intent to cause fear, or provoke violence. He had called three young Spanish women "*bloody foreigners*" and told them to "*go back to your own country*". In upholding the conviction, the House of Lords held that the expression 'racial group' in section 28(4) of the 1998 Act should be construed broadly. At paragraphs 9 and 10:

> "*... the definition of a racial group clearly goes beyond groups defined by their colour, race or ethnic origin. It encompasses both nationality (including citizenship) and national origins. This was quite deliberate. In Ealing London Borough Council v Race Relations Board [1972] AC 342, a majority of this House declined to interpret*

"national origins" in the list of prohibited grounds of discrimination under the Race Relations Act 1968 so as to include "nationality": discriminating against the non-British was allowed. Following this decision, the list of prohibited grounds was deliberately expanded in the Race Relations Act 1976 so as to include nationality. The list of grounds contained in the 1976 Act was adopted for the purposes of defining racial groups in the 1998 Act. An obvious advantage is that it helps to reduce argument about whether particular terms of abuse which are generally considered racist are or are not covered: does "Paki", for example, demonstrate hostility towards everyone who might hail from the Indian subcontinent or only towards citizens of Pakistan?

10. Nevertheless, it is argued for the appellant that the Act requires that the group be defined by what it is rather than by what it is not. Hence it is argued that Spaniards are covered but foreigners, that is the non-British, are not. The same argument would presumably be made about a person who showed hostility towards all non-whites, irrespective of the particular racial group to which they belonged. This cannot be right as a matter of language. Whether the group is defined exclusively by reference to what its members are not or inclusively by reference to what they are, the criterion by which the group is defined – nationality or colour – is the same."

Thus, not only is the term 'racial group' to be broadly construed, but it is clear that the offender need not specify which racial group he is discriminating against. Calling someone a 'foreigner' could be enough to mark them out as part of a 'racial group' for the purposes of the offences – the offender need not then go on to specify that the victim is a Spaniard, a French person or a Nigerian person. On this same point, see *Attorney General's Reference No4 of 2004* [2005] EWCA Crim 889 – referred to in *Rogers*, *supra* – in which the Court of Appeal held that an immigrant to the United Kingdom, who was therefore not British, could be a member of a 'racial group' for the purpose of the offences. In addition, in *DPP v M* (2004) EWCA 1453, the Divisional Court held that the phrase "*bloody foreigners*" could demonstrate hostility towards a racial group.

In *White* [2001] EWCA Crim 216, the appellant submitted that calling his victim an 'African bitch' did not involve an imputation of membership of a racial group, as Africa covered people from diverse cultural traditions. In dismissing the appeal, the Court held that although the word 'African' was outside the definition of an ethnic group, it came within the definition of a racial group and, given the context in which it had been used, there had been a racial connotation.

Members of the Romany and Irish travelling community are members of a racial group for these purposes. Romany gypsies have long been recognised as a racial group (*Commission for Racial Equality v Dutton* (1989) QB 783). Irish travellers have been recognised by the County Courts as members of an ethnic racial group for the purpose of the Race Relations Act 1976 (*O'Leary v Punch Retail*, Westminster County Court, 29 August 2000). There seems to be no reason why this would not extend to the definition of racial grouping in the criminal law.

In certain cases, a person's religious beliefs and racial identity may be tied closely together. In those circumstances, whether a particular crime is a racial or religious hate crime may be extremely context dependent. For example, the House of Lords in *Mandla v Dowell-Lee* (1983) 2 AC 548 held that Sikhs constituted a 'racial group' for the purposes of the Race Relations Act 1976. *Mandla* was applied in *R v JFS* (2009) UKSC 15, which held that a Jewish school's admission test of matrilineal descent from a Jewish woman was a test of ethnic origin, and so racially discriminatory rather than religious. As far back as 1980, the Employment Tribunal held that anti-Semitic comments were made to a fellow worker because he was a member of the Jewish race, rather than because of his religion (*Seide v Gillette Industries Ltd* (1980) IRLR 427). Although these are civil cases, again there would seem to be no reason why their reasoning would not extend to the criminal law.

Of course, unlike the Race Relations Act 1976, the criminal legislation does now allow protection to those discriminated against on the basis of their religion. It may be, then, that in practical terms the distinction is an artificial one. Where the context specifically points to a more obvious grouping than another, though, the prosecution should be brought on that basis, to aid clarity and avoid confusion.

Finally, the fact that the defendant might be of the same racial group as their victim is immaterial to the question of whether they have committed an aggravated offence (*White*, *supra*).

What Constitutes Disability?

Section 146 of the 2003 Act is the only legislative provision that deals with hate crimes on the basis of disability, or presumed disability; it mandates a sentencing uplift for offences that involve hostility based on disability, or presumed disability, or the victim.

Section 146(5) defines 'disability' as: "*any physical or mental impairment*".

As with 'racial group' and 'religious group', the legislation provides a broad scope for the definition of 'disability'. There is no set list of qualifying disabilities, or a requirement as to the visibility of the impairment. This must be correct; any such list would undoubtedly miss something out. Equally, the ever-evolving nature of medicine and discovery means that new impairments might be discovered that were previously unknown. In a similar vein, any requirement for visibility of disability would unjustly ignore the people targeted for a variety of invisible impairments. The requirement that the offence be motivated by hostility towards the person based on their disability, or that the offender demonstrate such hostility, is sufficient for the Prosecution to demonstrate a link between the disability and the offence, without the disability needing to be obvious.

What Constitutes Sexual Orientation?

'Sexual orientation' exclusively refers to the gender towards which the person is attracted, i.e. whether they are heterosexual, bisexual or homosexual – it does not extend further. This reflects the everyday definition of 'sexual orientation' in the Oxford English Dictionary, and the definition in the Equality Act 2010. (*B* [2013] EWCA Crim 291).

It follows that 'sexual orientation' should not be extended to cover a proclivity to certain sexual practices. So, for example, a person facing hostility because they enjoy unconventional sexual activity does not fall under the protections of the hate crime legislation.

What Constitutes Transgender Identity?

Again, section 146 of the 2003 Act is the only legislative provision that deals with hate crimes on the basis of transgender identity. Section 146(6) states:

> "*In this section references to being transgender include references to being transsexual, or undergoing, proposing to undergo or having undergone a process or part of a process of gender reassignment.*"

We can see from this that being transgender does not only apply to the stage at which the victim has completed a process of gender reassignment. It extends from the stage at which the victim is proposing to undergo gender reassignment. This makes sense when we consider that there is no logical reason why an offender who feels hostility towards a person who has undergone gender reassignment would not feel that same hostility towards a person who plans to undergo that reassignment.

CHAPTER FOUR
THE STATUTORY OFFENCES

This section analyses the statutory offences in more detail, further to the broad overview of chapter two and the analysis of key concepts throughout the law of hate crime in chapter three. It sets out each statutory offence, analyses its particular provisions and considers any guidance as to application and sentencing.

The Crime and Disorder Act 1998

Section 28 of the Crime and Disorder Act 1998

Section 28 of the Crime and Disorder Act 1998 sets out the meaning of 'racially or religiously aggravated', and applies not only to the offences under sections 29 to 32 of the 1998 Act, but also to those offences to which sections 145 and 146 of the Criminal Justice Act 2003 apply (see Chapter 5). In full, it states:

> "***28.— Meaning of "racially or religiously aggravated".***
>
> *(1) An offence is racially or religiously aggravated for the purposes of sections 29 to 32 below if—*
>
> > *(a) at the time of committing the offence, or immediately before or after doing so, the offender demonstrates towards the victim of the offence hostility based on the victim's membership (or presumed membership) of a racial or religious group ; or*
> >
> > *(b) the offence is motivated (wholly or partly) by hostility towards members of a racial or religious group based on their membership of that group.*

(2) In subsection (1)(a) above—

"membership", in relation to a racial or religious group, includes association with members of that group;

"presumed" means presumed by the offender.

(3) It is immaterial for the purposes of paragraph (a) or (b) of subsection (1) above whether or not the offender's hostility is also based, to any extent, on any other factor not mentioned in that paragraph.

(4) In this section "racial group" means a group of persons defined by reference to race, colour, nationality (including citizenship) or ethnic or national origins.

(5) In this section "religious group" means a group of persons defined by reference to religious belief or lack of religious belief."

In broad terms, the key elements are:

i. The offender must demonstrate hostility or be motivated by hostility towards the victim of the offence due to their membership, or presumed membership, of a racial or religious group;

ii. It is immaterial whether the offender's hostility is based, to any extent, on any other factor;

iii. The section defines 'racial group' and 'religious group';

iv. 'Membership' of a racial or religious group includes association with members of that group.

These concepts apply across the study of hate crime, and are crucial to understanding the law. They are, therefore, analysed separately in some detail in Chapter 3, and so I will not repeat that analysis here. Instead, we will go on to consider the statutory offences themselves.

Section 29 of the Crime and Disorder Act 1998

Section 29 of the 1998 Act sets out three offences of racially or religiously aggravated assault: (i) racially or religiously aggravated wounding; (ii) racially or religiously aggravated assault occasioning actual bodily harm; (iii) racially or religiously aggravated common assault.

Section 29 states:

> "***29.— Racially or religiously aggravated assaults.***
>
> *(1) A person is guilty of an offence under this section if he commits—*
>
> > *(a) an offence under section 20 of the Offences Against the Person Act 1861 (malicious wounding or grievous bodily harm);*
> >
> > *(b) an offence under section 47 of that Act (actual bodily harm); or*
> >
> > *(c) common assault,*
>
> *which is racially or religiously aggravated for the purposes of this section.*
>
> *(2) A person guilty of an offence falling within subsection (1)(a) or (b) above shall be liable—*
>
> > *(a) on summary conviction, to imprisonment for a term not exceeding six months or to a fine not exceeding the statutory maximum, or to both;*
> >
> > *(b) on conviction on indictment, to imprisonment for a term not exceeding seven years or to a fine, or to both.*
>
> *(3) A person guilty of an offence falling within subsection (1)(c) above shall be liable—*

(a) on summary conviction, to imprisonment for a term not exceeding six months or to a fine not exceeding the statutory maximum, or to both;

(b) on conviction on indictment, to imprisonment for a term not exceeding two years or to a fine, or to both."

Mode of Trial

All three offences under section 29 of the 1998 Act are either way offences. Therefore, they can be tried in the Magistrates' Court or the Crown Court. By comparison, whilst the corresponding 'basic' offences under sections 29(1)(a) and 29(1)(b) above are either way offences (section 20 wounding and assault occasioning actual bodily harm), the corresponding 'basic' offence of common assault is a summary only offence. Therefore it may only be tried in the Magistrates' Court.

Elements of the Offence

The Prosecution must prove the offence of assault, and then prove that the racial or religious aggravation was present. To prove an offence under section 29(1)(a), then, the Prosecution must first prove that an offence contrary to section 20 of the Offences Against the Person Act 1861 has been committed by the defendant. To prove an offence under section 29(1)(b), the Prosecution must first prove that an offence under section 47 of the Offences Against the Person Act 1861 has been committed by the defendant. To prove an offence under section 29(1)(c), the Prosecution must first prove that a common assault (or 'assault by beating') has been committed by the defendant.

Alternative Verdicts

The Crown Court has the power to return alternative verdicts to the Counts on the Indictment in certain circumstances; the Magistrates' Court has no such power. However, the circumstances in which alternative verdicts can be returned depend on the basic offence, and whether it can be tried on Indictment or is summary only.

Section 6(3) of the Criminal Law Act 1967 ("the 1967 Act") allows for alternative verdicts in trials on Indictment where the allegation includes (expressly or by implication) another offence falling within the jurisdiction of the court of trial. So a verdict of simple assault occasioning actual bodily harm contrary to section 47 of the Offences Against the Person Act 1861 can be returned as an alternative to a count of racially or religiously aggravated assault occasioning actual bodily harm, without it being included as a separate Count on the Indictment. The same applies to the basic and aggravated forms of wounding.

However, the basic offence of common assault does not fall within the jurisdiction of the Crown Court, so is not caught by section 6(3) of the 1967 Act.

It is then that section 40 of the Criminal Justice Act 1988 ("the 1988 Act") applies. Sections 40(1) and (2) of that Act state:

> "***40. Power to join in indictment count for common assault etc.***
>
> *(1) A count charging a person with a summary offence to which this section applies may be included in an indictment if the charge—*
>
> > *(a) is founded on the same facts or evidence as a count charging an indictable offence; or*
> >
> > *(b) is part of a series of offences of the same or similar character as an indictable offence which is also charged,*
>
> *but only if (in either case) the facts or evidence relating to the offence are disclosed by material which, in pursuance of regulations made under paragraph 1 of Schedule 3 to the Crime and Disorder Act 1998 (procedure where person sent for trial under section 51, has been served on the person charged.*

> *(2) Where a count charging an offence to which this section applies is included in an indictment, the offence shall be tried in the same manner as if it were an indictable offence; but the Crown Court may only deal with the offender in respect of it in a manner in which a magistrates' court could have dealt with him."*

Section 40(3) of the 1988 Act lists common assault as one of the offences to which the section applies.

Therefore, common assault may be an alternative verdict to the aggravated form, but must be included in the Indictment as an alternative. This approach has been affirmed by the Court of Appeal; without common assault being expressly included as an alternative, the only option available to the jury is the aggravated form (*Clifford* [2003] EWCA Crim 3630).

If the accused is charged with alternative offences and pleads not guilty to both, it would be 'unfair and disproportionate' to convict of both. In *Dyer v Watford Magistrates Court* [2013] EWHC 547 (Admin), the magistrates were held to have wrongly convicted the accused of the racially aggravated and simple forms of a public order offence. The correct approach was to record no verdict on the lesser charge and adjourn it without setting a date; this would ensure that if the accused appealed successfully against the conviction for the more serious offence, the lesser offence can be brought back, if appropriate.

Sentencing

All offences under section 29 of the 1998 Act carry higher maximum penalties than their basic counterparts. The maximum penalty on Indictment for sections 29(1)(a) and (b) is seven years' imprisonment. The maximum penalty on Indictment for section 29(1)(c) is two years' imprisonment.

The Sentencing Council's Definitive Guideline on Assault addresses the aggravated offences alongside their corresponding basic offences.

The Court of Appeal, in Saunders (2000) 1 Cr App R 458 emphasised that the courts must give effect to the will of Parliament to ensure that prejudice is not allowed to flourish, by imposing more severe sentences for the aggravated offences. At paragraph 13: "*Those who indulge in racially aggravated violence must expect to be punished severely, in order to discourage the repetition of that behaviour, by them or others.*" It would be helpful if the sentencing judge first considered the appropriate sentence for the offence in the absence of racial aggravation, and then add a further term for the racial element. Even where the basic offence would not cross the custodial threshold, the element of racial aggravation might result in the custody threshold being passed.

An example of a case where the racial aggravation pushed the sentence over the custodial threshold is Slater [2005] EWCA Crim 2882, where a sentence of four months' imprisonment was held to be appropriate for a racially aggravated common assault. The assault (which comprised of threatening with a clenched fist) did not merit a custodial sentence, but the racial aggravation was sufficient to take the offence across the custodial threshold.

Where the racially aggravated form of the offence has not been included on the Indictment, it is open to the Sentencing Judge to find (to the criminal standard) that the offence is in fact so aggravated and sentence accordingly. However, this does not mean that the Prosecution is relieved of its duty to consider the Indictment with care; in the majority of cases where the evidence supports an aggravated form of assault, it should be placed on the Indictment (O'Leary [2015] EWCA Crim 1306).

Section 30 of the Crime and Disorder Act 1998

Section 30 of the 1998 Act deals with offences of racially and religiously aggravated criminal damage. The basic offence is that found in section 1(1) of the Criminal Damage Act 1971 (destroying or damaging property belonging to another).

Section 30 states, in full:

> "***30.— Racially or religiously aggravated criminal damage.***
>
> *(1) A person is guilty of an offence under this section if he commits an offence under section 1(1) of the Criminal Damage Act 1971 (destroying or damaging property belonging to another) which is racially or religiously aggravated for the purposes of this section.*
>
> *(2) A person guilty of an offence under this section shall be liable—*
>
> > *(a) on summary conviction, to imprisonment for a term not exceeding six months or to a fine not exceeding the statutory maximum, or to both;*
> >
> > *(b) on conviction on indictment, to imprisonment for a term not exceeding fourteen years or to a fine, or to both.*
>
> *(3) For the purposes of this section, section 28(1)(a) above shall have effect as if the person to whom the property belongs or is treated as belonging for the purposes of that Act were the victim of the offence.*"

Mode of Trial

The offence under section 30 of the 1998 Act is an either way offence, and so can be tried in the Magistrates' Court or the Crown Court. Similarly, basic criminal damage is generally triable either way. However, where the value of the property alleged to have been destroyed or the value of the alleged damage is not more than £5,000, the simple offence is treated as if it were triable only summarily (see section 22 of and Schedule 2 to the Magistrates' Courts Act 1980)

Elements of the Offence

As with the other statutory offences, the Prosecution must prove the basic offence and the racial or religious aggravation (as defined by section 28 of the 1998 Act). In this case, then, the Prosecution must prove that the defendant: (i) without lawful excuse damaged or destroyed property belonging to another, either with the intent to destroy or damage that property or being reckless as to whether it would be damaged; (ii) that the defendant either demonstrated racial or religious hostility at the time of the offence, or immediately before or after; or that the defendant was motivated by racial or religious hostility.

Section 28 requires that the hostility is directed towards the victim's membership or presumed membership of a racial or religious group. Clearly, the property being damaged does not have a race or religion. For this reason, section 30(3) of the 1998 Act provides that the victim shall be deemed to be the owner (or the person who is treated as the owner) of the property.

Alternative Verdicts

See the 'alternative verdicts' section under the heading 'Section 29 of the Crime and Disorder Act 1998' above, for more detail.

As set out in those paragraphs, section 6(3) of the 1967 Act allows the Crown Court to return a guilty verdict to a lesser offence as an alternative to the offence on the Indictment under certain circumstances. However, the lesser offence must be triable in the Crown Court. This would apply to criminal damage where the damage caused is valued at over £5,000.

Section 40 of the 1988 Act allows certain named summary only offences to be alternative verdicts on an Indictment, but a specific Count alleging that offence must be included in the Indictment. The summary only version of criminal damage is included in this list. Therefore, where the damage caused is valued at under £5,000, the basic version of criminal damage may be included as an alternative Count, but must be expressly included on the Indictment.

If the accused is charged with alternative offences and pleads not guilty to both, it would be 'unfair and disproportionate' to convict of both. See *Dyer v Watford Magistrates Court*, *supra*.

Sentencing

The maximum penalty on Indictment is fourteen years' imprisonment. The maximum penalty on summary conviction is six months' imprisonment.

As of October 2019, the Sentencing Council has issued guidelines for sentencing criminal damage in both the Crown Court and the Magistrates' Court, including offences of racially and religiously aggravated criminal damage. The guidelines are divided between those where the value exceeds £5,000 and those where the value falls below £5,000.

With regards to racial and religious aggravation, the guidelines distinguish between factors indicating a low level of aggravation, factors indicating a medium level of aggravation and factors indicating a high level of aggravation.

Factors indicating a low level of aggravation include: (i) the aggravated element formed a minimal part of the offence as a whole; (ii) there was little or no impact on the victim or victim's family.

Factors indicating a medium level of aggravation include: (i) the aggravation formed a significant proportion of the offence as a whole; (ii) the aggravated nature of the offence caused some distress to the victim or the victim's family.

Finally, factors indicating a high level of aggravation include: (i) the racial or religious aggravation was the predominant motive for the offence; (ii) the aggravated nature of the offence caused severe distress to the victim or victim's family; and (iii) the offender was a member of, or associated with, a group promoting hostility based on race or religion.

The relevant sentencing caselaw falls before the recent Guidelines, so is of limited use to that extent; the Guidelines will always take precedent in the sentencing Court. However, the following case may be of some interest when considering the ways in which the courts have tackled the relationship between the basic and the aggravated offences. In *O'Brien* (2003) EWCA Crim 302, a custodial sentence of 14 months' imprisonment had been imposed for racially aggravated criminal damage. The appellant's neighbours were a group of asylum seekers. The appellant had thrown bricks through the windows of their house when they were at home, and attacked a car he thought belonged to them. Whilst committing the offences, the appellant had shouted racial abuse. The sentencing judge had imposed two months' imprisonment for the basic offence, and uplifted the sentence by 12 months for the racial aggravation.

Allowing the appeal, the Court accepted that the sentencing guidance on hate crimes indicated an uplift of 40 to 70 per cent to the sentence for the basic offence. However, this was not an inflexible rule; in the present case, the Court held that the mere application of a percentage to the two-month sentence would not fairly reflect the seriousness of the offence. The racial motivation made the case far more serious than a case of criminal damage appropriate to a two-month sentence. Notwithstanding that assessment, the 14-month sentence of imprisonment was too great. A sentence of six months' imprisonment was substituted.

Section 31 of the Crime and Disorder Act 1998

Section 31 of the 1998 Act creates racially and religiously aggravated public order offences. It states:

> "*31. Racially or religiously aggravated public order offences.*
>
> *(1) A person is guilty of an offence under this section if he commits—*
>
> > *(a) an offence under section 4 of the Public Order Act 1986 (fear or provocation of violence);*
> >
> > *(b) an offence under section 4A of that Act (intentional harassment, alarm or distress); or*
> >
> > *(c) an offence under section 5 of that Act (harassment, alarm or distress),*
> >
> > *which is racially or religiously aggravated for the purposes of this section.*
>
> *[...]*
>
> *(4) A person guilty of an offence falling within subsection (1)(a) or (b) above shall be liable—*
>
> > *(a) on summary conviction, to imprisonment for a term not exceeding six months or to a fine not exceeding the statutory maximum, or to both;*
> >
> > *(b) on conviction on indictment, to imprisonment for a term not exceeding two years or to a fine, or to both.*
>
> *(5) A person guilty of an offence falling within subsection (1)(c) above shall be liable on summary conviction to a fine not exceeding level 4 on the standard scale.*

(6) If, on the trial on indictment of a person charged with an offence falling within subsection (1)(a) or (b) above, the jury find him not guilty of the offence charged, they may find him guilty of the basic offence mentioned in that provision.

(7) For the purposes of subsection (1)(c) above, section 28(1)(a) above shall have effect as if the person likely to be caused harassment, alarm or distress were the victim of the offence."

Mode of Trial

The offences under section 31(1)(a) and 31(1)(b) of the 1998 Act are either way offences, so can be tried in the Magistrates' Court or the Crown Court. By comparison, their basic counterparts are summary only offences.

Section 31(1)(c) is, like its basic counterpart, triable only summarily.

Elements of the Offence

The Prosecution will need to prove the elements of the basic offence, and then prove the racial or religious aggravation.

For an offence under section 31(1)(a) of the 1998 Act, the Prosecution will need to prove:

i. The defendant used threatening, abusive or insulting words or behaviour towards another person;

ii. The defendant did so with intent to cause the person to believe that immediate unlawful violence would be used against that person or another by any person; or with intent to provoke the immediate use of unlawful violence by that person or another; or where that person is likely to believe that such violence would be used; or where it is likely that such violence will be provoked;

iii. The words or behaviour were used in a public or private place, but not a dwelling house;

iv. At the time of doing so, or immediately before or after doing so, the defendant demonstrated hostility based on the victim's membership of a racial or religious group; or

v. The defendant was motivated by hostility based one the victim's membership of a racial or religious group.

For an offence under section 31(1)(b) of the 1998 Act, the Prosecution will need to prove:

i. That the defendant used threatening, abusive or insulting words or behaviour, or disorderly behaviour;

ii. That the defendant intended to cause, and thereby caused, harassment, alarm or distress;

iii. The conduct was in a public or private place, but not a dwelling house;

iv. That at the time of doing so, or immediately before or after doing so, the defendant demonstrated hostility based on the victim's membership of a racial or religious group; or

v. The defendant was motivated by hostility based one the victim's membership of a racial or religious group.

Finally, for an offence under section 31(1)(c) of the 1998 Act, the Prosecution will need to prove:

i. That the defendant used threatening or abusive words or behaviour or disorderly behaviour;

ii. That the defendant had the intention or awareness that the behaviour may be threatening, abusive or disorderly;

iii. That the offence took place in public or private, but not in a dwelling;

iv. That the conduct was within the hearing or sight of a person likely to be caused harassment, alarm or distress;

v. That at the time of doing so, or immediately before or after doing so, the defendant demonstrated hostility based on the victim's membership of a racial or religious group; or

vi. The defendant was motivated by hostility based one the victim's membership of a racial or religious group.

With regards to section 31(1)(c) of the 1998 Act, the basic offence (section 5 of the Public Order Act 1986) does not have a 'victim' – it is committed simply by committing the conduct within the hearing or sight of a person likely to be caused harassment, alarm or distress. However, to prove aggravation, the Prosecution must prove hostility on the basis of the victim's membership of a racial or religious group. Section 31(7) therefore provides that the 'victim' in section 31(1)(c) of the 1998 Act is deemed to be the person who is likely to be caused harassment, alarm or distress.

All the offences can be committed in a public or private place, but no offence is committed when inside a dwelling. Section 8 of the Public Order Act 1986 defines a 'dwelling' as "*any structure or part of a structure occupied as a person's home or as other living accommodation*". In *DPP v D* [2017] EWHC 2244 (Admin), the High Court held that being 'inside a dwelling' did not extend to include being inside its garden. Accordingly, the Respondent – who had been inside her grandmother's garden when she yelled a racially aggravated comment to a Polish couple in the neighbouring garden – had committed a public order offence under section 31 of the 1998 Act, and the DPP's appeal against her acquittal was allowed.

Alternative Verdicts

Section 6(3) of the Criminal Law Act 1967 provides that alternative verdicts can be returned in the Crown Court where the lesser offence would also be triable in the Crown Court. Magistrates' Courts cannot return alternative verdicts.

That does not apply to the basic versions of the offences in section 31 of the 1998 Act, which are summary only offences.

Section 40 of the Criminal Justice Act 1988 sets out a number of summary only offences that may be included as alternative Counts on a Crown Court Indictment. The public order offences under sections 4, 4A and 5 of the Public Order Act 1986 are not included.

Section 31 of the 1998 Act itself deals with this problem. By section 31(6) of that Act, a person acquitted of the aggravated offences under sections 31(1)(a) or 31(1)(b) may nevertheless be convicted of the basic versions of those offences.

Section 31 explicitly states that the jury may find the defendant guilty of the lesser offence only where they have found him not guilty of the aggravated offence. Therefore, where a jury has been discharged following a successful application to stay proceedings as an abuse of process, or because it has not been able to reach a verdict, the jury cannot return a verdict of guilty to a lesser offence – as there has been no not guilty verdict from the jury. (*Khela* [2005] EWCA Crim 3446).

Section 31(1)(c) is triable only summarily. Given that the Magistrates' Courts have no power to reach alternative verdicts, a person acquitted of that aggravated offence cannot then be found guilty of the basic version. It is not open to the Magistrates' Court to record convictions for both the simple and racially aggravated forms of a public order offence arising from the same incident (*R (on the application of Dyer) v Watford Magistrates' Court* [2013] EWHC 547 (Admin)).

If the accused is charged with alternative offences and pleads not guilty to both, it would be 'unfair and disproportionate' to convict of both. See Dyer v Watford Magistrates Court, *supra*

Sentencing

The maximum penalty for offences under section 31(1)(a) and 31(1)(b) is two years' imprisonment. The maximum penalty for an offence under section 31(1)(c) is six months' imprisonment. There are no sentencing guidelines for offences under the 1998 Act.

In *Duffy* [2000] 11 WLUK 620, the Court found that a twelve-month sentence for an offence under section 31 of the 1998 Act was excessive, where there had been a guilty plea and a finding that the defendant did not harbour racist views.

Section 32 of the Crime and Disorder Act 1998

Section 32 of the 1998 Act deals with racially or religiously aggravated harassment and stalking. It creates four aggravated offences, and states:

> "***32. Racially or religiously aggravated harassment etc.***
>
> *(1) A person is guilty of an offence under this section if he commits—*
>
> > *(a) an offence under section 2 or 2A of the Protection from Harassment Act 1997 (offences of harassment and stalking); or*
> >
> > *(b) an offence under section 4 or 4A of that Act (putting people in fear of violence and stalking involving fear of violence or serious alarm or distress), which is racially or religiously aggravated for the purposes of this section.*
>
> *[…]*
>
> *(3) A person guilty of an offence falling within subsection (1)(a) above shall be liable—*

(a) on summary conviction, to imprisonment for a term not exceeding six months or to a fine not exceeding the statutory maximum, or to both;

(b) on conviction on indictment, to imprisonment for a term not exceeding two years or to a fine, or to both.

(4) A person guilty of an offence falling within subsection (1)(b) above shall be liable—

(a) on summary conviction, to imprisonment for a term not exceeding six months or to a fine not exceeding the statutory maximum, or to both;

(b) on conviction on indictment, to imprisonment for a term not exceeding 14 years or to a fine, or to both.

(5) If, on the trial on indictment of a person charged with an offence falling within subsection (1)(a) above, the jury find him not guilty of the offence charged, they may find him guilty of either basic offence mentioned in that provision.

(6) If, on the trial on indictment of a person charged with an offence falling within subsection (1)(b) above, the jury find him not guilty of the offence charged, they may find him guilty of an offence falling within subsection (1)(a) above."

Mode of Trial

All the offences created by section 32 are triable either way, so can be heard in the Magistrates' Court or the Crown Court. By contrast, the basic versions of the offences are a combination of summary only and either way offences.

The basic offence of harassment under section 2 of the Protection from Harassment Act 1997 is triable only in the Magistrates' Court. Similarly, the basic offence of stalking under section 2A of the same Act is triable only in the Magistrates' Court.

The basic offences under sections 4 and 4A of the Protection from Harassment Act 1997 are, however, triable either way.

Elements of the Offences

The Prosecution will need to prove the elements of the basic offences, and then prove that the defendant either demonstrated the requisite hostility, or was motivated by the requisite hostility.

To prove an offence under section 32(1)(a), the Prosecution will need to prove:

i. That the defendant committed an offence of harassment (section 2 of the Protection from Harassment Act 1997) or stalking (section 2A of the Protection from Harassment Act 1997);

ii. That the defendant demonstrated hostility towards the victim of the offence based on his race or religion; or

iii. That the defendant was motivated, at least in part, by hostility based on a racial or religious grouping.

To prove an offence under section 32(1)(b), the Prosecution will need to prove:

i. That the defendant committed an offence of putting people in fear of violence (section 4 of the Protection from Harassment Act 1997) or stalking involving fear of violence or serious alarm or distress (section 4A of the Protection from Harassment Act 1997);

ii. That the defendant demonstrated hostility towards the victim of the offence based on his race or religion; or

iii. That the defendant was motivated, at least in part, by hostility based on a racial or religious grouping.

Alternative Verdicts

Section 6(3) of the Criminal Law Act 1967 provides that alternative verdicts can be returned in the Crown Court where the lesser offence would also be triable in the Crown Court. Magistrates' Courts cannot return alternative verdicts.

Therefore, on a trial for an offence under section 32(1)(b) of the 1998 Act, the jury may find the defendant not guilty, but find the defendant guilty of the basic version of the offence under sections 4 or 4A of the Protection from Harassment Act 1997.

However, sections 2 and 2A of the Protection from Harassment Act 1997 (the basic counterparts to section 32(1)(a) of the 1998 Act) are triable only summarily. Section 6(3) of the Criminal Law Act 1967 does not, therefore, apply to those offences.

It is for this reason that section 32 explicitly provides that on a trial for an offence under section 32(1)(a) of the 1998 Act, the jury may find the defendant not guilty, but may find the defendant guilty of the basic version of the offence under section 2 or 2A of the Protection from Harassment Act 1997.

Section 32(6) also provides that on a trial for an offence under section 32(1)(b) of the 1998 Act, the jury may find the defendant not guilty, but may find the defendant guilty of an offence under section 32(1)(a) of the 1998 Act as an alternative.

If the accused is charged with alternative offences and pleads not guilty to both, it would be 'unfair and disproportionate' to convict of both. See *Dyer v Watford Magistrates Court*, *supra*

Sentencing

The maximum term of imprisonment for an offence under section 32(1)(a) is two years' imprisonment. The maximum term of imprisonment for an offence under section 32(1)(b) is 14 years' imprisonment. There are no sentencing guidelines for offences under the 1998 Act.

In *Fawthrop* [2017] EWCA Crim 1500, the Court of Appeal gave guidance as to the factors relevant when sentencing an offence under section 32 of the 1998 Act.

The Court listed the following as relevant to culpability:

i. Whether there had been disobedience with a court order;

ii. The seriousness of the conduct;

iii. The number of incidents in the course of conduct;

iv. Whether others were used as part of the course of conduct;

v. The offender's mental health.

The Court also noted that the Magistrates' Court sentencing guidelines listed two features that may indicate lower culpability: (i) an offender's limited understanding of the effect on the victim; (ii) initial provocation.

The Court listed the following factors as relevant to harm:

i. The effect on the victims and whether they needed medical treatment or counselling;

ii. The persistence in the offending (although this does overlap with culpability).

The Court stated that once culpability and harm had been assessed, it should indicate what sentence would have been passed absent the racially aggravating factors. It was clear, then, that a racially or religiously aggravated offence was to be treated as a more serious offence than the basic one, given that the maximum sentence for the aggravated version is higher. In that case, a low level community sentence was unduly lenient, but the Court did not alter it, given the Respondent's mitigation and the fact that the sentencing Judge had given her an unsolicited indication that she would not go to prison if she were to plead guilty.

The Public Order Act 1986

Part III of the Public Order Act 1986 creates offences of incitement to racial hatred, and Part 3A creates offences of incitement to hatred on the grounds of religion or sexual orientation. Sections 18 to 23 of the 1986 Act create offences relating to racial hatred. Sections 29B to 29G create offences relating to hatred on the grounds of religion or sexual orientation. As a broad description, it prohibits various forms of expression, including speech, the written word and production of a play.

Freedom of expression is a protected fundamental right under Article 10 of the European Convention on Human Rights. However, it is not an absolute right, meaning that it can be limited in certain circumstances. This includes where the restriction is prescribed by law and is necessary in a democratic society – the 1986 Act would seem to fall within these caveats.

Additionally, section 29J of the 1986 Act provides that nothing in Part 3A of the 1986 Act should be read or given effect in a way that, essentially, prohibits freedom of expression in relation to religious belief. It protects discussion, criticism, expressions of antipathy, dislike, ridicule, insult or abuse of particular religions or the beliefs or practices of their adherents, or of any other belief system or its adherents, or urging adherents of a different religion or belief system to cease their practice of that religion or belief system.

Section 29JA similarly seeks to explicitly protect expression about certain aspects of sexual orientation. It provides that discussion or criticism of sexual conduct, or the urging of persons to refrain from or modify such conduct or practices, shall not be taken of itself as threatening or intended to stir up hatred. It also explicitly states that discussion or criticism of marriage which concerns the sex of the parties to marriage shall not be taken, of itself, to be threatening or intended to stir up hatred.

Offences by a Corporation

Sections 28 and 29M address the situation where a corporation is alleged to have committed an offence under Parts III or 3A (respectively) of the 1986 Act.

Section 28 provides that where a body corporate is guilty of an offence under Part III of the 1986 Act, and it is shown that the offence was committed with the consent or connivance of a director, manager, secretary or other similar officer of the body – or a person purporting to act in such a capacity – both that person and the body corporate are guilty of the offence. Where the affairs of the body corporate are managed by its members, the provision will apply to the member's management functions as it applies to a director.

Section 29M sets out the exact same provisions, in relation to offences under Part 3A of the 1986 Act.

Mode of Trial of the Offences under the 1986 Act

By virtue of section 27 of the 1986 Act, all offences in sections 18 to 23 are triable either way. Under section 29L of the 1986 Act, the complementary offences in sections 29B to 29G are triable either way also.

Statutory Sentencing Provisions

Sections 27 and 29L of the 1986 Act set out the statutory maximum punishments for offences under sections 18 to 23, and 29B to 29G. There are no Guidelines. Where there are cases of interest to a particular offence, I have set those out in the relevant section for each offence.

A person convicted of any of the offences under sections 18 to 23 of the 1968 Act faces a maximum term of seven years' imprisonment in the Crown Court, and six months' imprisonment in the Magistrates' Court (section 27 of the 1986 Act).

A person convicted of any of the offences under sections 29B to 29G faces a maximum term of seven years' imprisonment in the Crown Court, and 12 months' imprisonment in the Magistrates' Court (section 29L of the 1986 Act).

Sections 17, 29A and 29AB of the Public Order Act 1986

Section 17 of the 1986 Act sets out the definition of 'racial hatred':

> *"In this Part "racial hatred" means hatred against a group of persons . . . defined by reference to colour, race, nationality (including citizenship) or ethnic or national origins."*

So we can see, again, that 'race' is defined broadly – by reference to colour, race, nationality (including citizenship, ethnic or national origin. The word 'hostility', which we see repeated throughout the relevant provisions of the Crime and Disorder Act 1998 and the Criminal Justice Act 2003, has been replaced by 'hatred'. Taking the ordinary meaning of both words, the latter would appear to be a higher threshold.

The offences under Part III of the 1986 Act are designed to tackle incitement to racial hatred. In general terms, the defendant will be guilty of an offence under this Part if she or he: a) commits an action described in the relevant section; b) the action must be threatening, abusive or insulting; and c) it must be intended to, or likely in all the circumstances, stir up racial hatred.

A point to note is the phrase 'likely in all the circumstances'; in other words, racial hatred must be more than a mere possibility. Whether something is 'likely' to stir up racial hatred may well be extremely context dependent. In particular, the likely audience may well be relevant when considering the consequences of the defendant's action.

Section 29A sets out the meaning of 'religious hatred':

> *"29A. Meaning of "religious hatred"*
>
> *In this Part "religious hatred" means hatred against a group of persons defined by reference to religious belief or lack of religious belief*".

This interpretation mimics that elsewhere in the legislation: hostility on the grounds of religious belief does not just encompass a belief in a particular religion, but also lack of religious belief. Therefore, the atheist who finds themselves the victim of a crime that demonstrates hostility towards them as an atheist, or is motivated by such hostility, should be able to avail themselves of the legislative protections.

Section 29AB sets out the meaning of hatred on the grounds of sexual orientation:

> ***"29AB. Meaning of "hatred on the grounds of sexual orientation"***
>
> *In this Part "hatred on the grounds of sexual orientation" means hatred against a group of persons defined by reference to sexual orientation (whether towards persons of the same sex, the opposite sex or both)."*

This section makes it clear that 'sexual orientation' refers to the gender of the person to whom one is attracted – there does not appear to be scope for it to be extended to cover sexual preferences. This reflects the interpretation of 'sexual orientation' in the caselaw governing section 146 of the Criminal Justice Act 2003 (see Chapter 5: 'Sentencing Uplift Provisions').

<u>Sections 18 and 29B of the Public Order Act 1986</u>

Sections 18 and 29B create an offence of using words or behaviour, or display of written material. Section 18 creates an offence in respect of racial hatred; section 29B creates a similar offence in relation to hatred on the grounds of religion or sexual orientation.

Section 18 states:

> ***"18 Use of words or behaviour or display of written material.***
>
> *(1) A person who uses threatening, abusive or insulting words or behaviour, or displays any written material which is threatening, abusive or insulting, is guilty of an offence if—*
>
> > *(a) he intends thereby to stir up racial hatred, or*
> >
> > *(b) having regard to all the circumstances racial hatred is likely to be stirred up thereby.*
>
> *(2) An offence under this section may be committed in a public or a private place, except that no offence is committed where the words or behaviour are used, or the written material is displayed, by a person*

inside a dwelling and are not heard or seen except by other persons in that or another dwelling.

[…]

(4) In proceedings for an offence under this section it is a defence for the accused to prove that he was inside a dwelling and had no reason to believe that the words or behaviour used, or the written material displayed, would be heard or seen by a person outside that or any other dwelling.

(5) A person who is not shown to have intended to stir up racial hatred is not guilty of an offence under this section if he did not intend his words or behaviour, or the written material, to be, and was not aware that it might be, threatening, abusive or insulting.

(6) This section does not apply to words or behaviour used, or written material displayed, solely for the purpose of being included in a programme [included in a programme service]."

Section 29B states:

"***29B. Use of words or behaviour or display of written material***

(1) A person who uses threatening words or behaviour, or displays any written material which is threatening, is guilty of an offence if he intends thereby to stir up religious hatred or hatred on the grounds of sexual orientation.

(2) An offence under this section may be committed in a public or a private place, except that no offence is committed where the words or behaviour are used, or the written material is displayed, by a person inside a dwelling and are not heard or seen except by other persons in that or another dwelling.

[…]

(4) In proceedings for an offence under this section it is a defence for the accused to prove that he was inside a dwelling and had no reason to believe that the words or behaviour used, or the written material displayed, would be heard or seen by a person outside that or any other dwelling.

(5) This section does not apply to words or behaviour used, or written material displayed, solely for the purpose of being included in a programme service."

Elements of the Offences

Under both sections 18 and 29B of the 1986 Act, the Prosecution will need to prove:

i. That a person used words, behaviour or displayed written material;

ii. That the words, behaviour or displayed material was threatening or (in the case of section 18) abusive or insulting;

iii. The person intended thereby to stir up racial hatred (section 18) or hatred on the grounds of religion or sexual orientation (section 29B); or

iv. In relation to section 18 only – that, having regard to all the circumstances, hatred on the basis of race was likely to be stirred up thereby;

The offence can be committed in either a private or a public place, but will not be committed where the relevant words, behaviour or written material was inside a dwelling, and not heard or seen except by other persons in that or another dwelling. Section 29 sets out the definition of a 'dwelling' for the purposes of Part III of the 1986 Act as:

> *"dwelling" means any structure or part of a structure occupied as a person's home or other living accommodation (whether the occupation is separate or shared with others) but does not include any part not so occupied, and for this purpose "structure" includes a tent, caravan, vehicle, vessel or other temporary or movable structure;"*

Sections 18(4) and 29B(4) set out identical statutory defences: it is a defence for the defendant to prove that he was inside a dwelling and had no reason to believe that his words, behaviour or the written material displayed, would be heard or seen by a person outside that or any other dwelling. The statutory defence thus prevents the potentially unjust situation where a person had no reason to believe that they would be heard or seen by anyone outside the dwelling, let alone intended anyone to hear or see them, but happens to be overheard or seen anyway – where they would not have been committing an offence had they not been overheard or seen, and there was clearly no knowledge that anybody else would be privy to the offensive actions. It prevents the existence of an offence turning on such happenstance.

Section 18(5) sets out an additional statutory defence, in relation to racial hatred. Section 18(1)(b) provides that an offence can be committed if racial hatred was likely to be stirred up in all the circumstances. There is no corresponding provision for section 29B – an offence can only be committed under that section where the defendant intends to stir up hatred based on religion or sexual orientation. So it is that section 18(5) provides a statutory defence that is applicable only to section 18(1)(b). Under section 18(5), the defendant is not to be found guilty if he can prove that he did not intend the words, behaviour or written material to be, <u>and</u> was not aware that it <u>might</u> be, threatening, abusive or insulting.

Finally, words, behaviour and written material that is used solely for the purpose of being included in a programme, that is included in a programme service, is exempt from forming an offence under these sections.

Sentencing Authorities

In *Saleem* [2007] EWCA Crim 2692 the Court of Appeal set out some factors to consider when sentencing inchoate offences, which included (in that case) stirring up racial hatred. Sentences should reflect the seriousness of the offending by taking into account:

i. How long it lasted;

ii. The sophistication;

iii. The skill and industry devoted to it; and

iv. The likelihood that it would lead, or had led, others to commit (in that case) acts of terrorism.

In *Burns* [2017] EWCA Crim 1466, the appellant was convicted of one Count of publishing written material contrary to section 19 of the 1986 Act (see below), and one Count of stirring up racial hatred contrary to section 18 of the 1986 Act. The first Count related to a series of racist posts on Facebook, particularly directed at Jewish and Afro-Caribbean communities. The second Count related to a speech made outside the United Sates' Embassy. In that speech, the appellant alleged that non-white immigrants were "rapists, robbers and murderers" and that Jewish people were "parasites and bankers" who wanted to create a "mongrelised" race. The speech was filmed and, with the appellant's knowledge, the video was posted on YouTube. On the first Count, the Court of Appeal considered a sentence of 18 months' imprisonment to be appropriate. On the second Count, the Court considered a sentence of twelve months' imprisonment to be appropriate.

Sections 19 and 29C of the Public Order Act 1986

Sections 19 and 29C address the publication or distribution of written material. Section 19 creates an offence in relation to racial hatred.

Section 29C creates an offence in relation to hatred on the grounds of religion or sexual orientation.

Section 19 states:

"***19 Publishing or distributing written material.***

(1) A person who publishes or distributes written material which is threatening, abusive or insulting is guilty of an offence if—

(a) he intends thereby to stir up racial hatred, or

(b) having regard to all the circumstances racial hatred is likely to be stirred up thereby.

(2) In proceedings for an offence under this section it is a defence for an accused who is not shown to have intended to stir up racial hatred to prove that he was not aware of the content of the material and did not suspect, and had no reason to suspect, that it was threatening, abusive or insulting.

(3) References in this Part to the publication or distribution of written material are to its publication or distribution to the public or a section of the public."

Section 29C states:

"***29C. Publishing or distributing written material***

(1) A person who publishes or distributes written material which is threatening is guilty of an offence if he intends thereby to stir up religious hatred or hatred on the grounds of sexual orientation.

(2) References in this Part to the publication or distribution of written material are to its publication or distribution to the public or a section of the public."

Elements of the Offences

Under both sections 19 and 29C of the 1986 Act, the Prosecution will need to prove:

i. That a person published or distributed written material;

ii. The written material was threatening or (in the case of section 19) abusive or insulting;

iii. The person intended to stir up racial hatred (section 19) or hatred on the grounds of religion or sexual orientation (section 29C); or

iv. In the case of section 19 only – that, having regard to all the circumstances, racial hatred was likely to be stirred up thereby;

v. The material was published or distributed to the public, or to a section of the public.

Sections 29 (applying to offences created by sections 18 to 23) and 29N (applying to offences created by sections 29B to 29G) of the 1986 Act define 'written material' as "*any sign or other visible representation*". It would seem, then, that symbols (such as, for example, a Nazi symbol) may be taken as falling within the ambit of sections 19 and 29C.

In a similar way to section 18(1)(b) of the 1986 Act, section 19(1)(b) allows the offence to be committed where the defendant did not intend to stir up racial hatred, but where racial hatred was likely to be stirred up, having regard to all the circumstances. There is, then, a statutory defence under section 19(2), where the prosecution is relying on section 19(1)(b). If the accused can prove that he was not aware of the content of the material and had no reason to suspect that it was threatening, abusive or insulting, nor had reason to suspect as such, then he will have a complete defence.

Sheppard [2010] EWCA Crim 65 highlights the increased role that the Internet plays in offences of this nature. In *Sheppard*, the appellants had created material casting doubt about the holocaust and containing derogatory remarks about various racial groups, and uploaded it to a website. The website was hosted by a remote server in California, so points of jurisdiction were argued. The Judge in that case, applying *Smith (Wallace Duncan) (No.4)* [2004] EWCA Crim 631, decided that the court had jurisdiction as a substantial measure of the appellants' activities had taken place in the United Kingdom; the Court of Appeal upheld that decision.

Sentencing Authorities

Bonehill-Paine [2016] EWCA Crim 980 identified the following factors as relevant to sentencing an offence under section 19 of the 1986 Act:

i. The nature of the publication and the intent behind it;

ii. The need to deter others;

iii. The number of people who saw the material; and

iv. The consequences of them having seen it.

In *Bonehill-Paine*, the appellant had published a post on his own Internet site encouraging people to attend a demonstration, described as an "anti Jewification event" which was to "liberate" Golders Green in North London as part of a "Summer of Hate". Included were anti-Jewish posters. A sentence of imprisonment of three years and 4 months was upheld.

In *Bitton* [2019] EWCA Crim 1372, concurrent sentences of two years and eight months' imprisonment were considered appropriate in the case of a man who was convicted of posting written material intending to stir up racial and religious hatred. He had posted 86 anti-immigration, pro-Brexit tweets, some of which referred to killing Muslims and Black people, in a six day period before the 2016 Brexit referendum.

In _Burns_, *supra*, the Court of Appeal considered a sentence of 18 months' imprisonment to be appropriate in a case where the appellant had posted a number of racist Facebook posts. (He was also sentenced to a consecutive term of 12 months' imprisonment for an offence under section 18 of the 1986 Act – as to which, see that section above).

Sections 20 and 29D of the Public Order Act 1986

Sections 20 and 29D of the 1986 Act create offences in relation to the public performance of a play. Section 20 creates an offence in relation to racial hatred. Section 29D creates an offence in relation to hatred on the grounds of religion or sexual orientation.

Section 20 states:

> "***20 Public performance of play.***
>
> *(1) If a public performance of a play is given which involves the use of threatening, abusive or insulting words or behaviour, any person who presents or directs the performance is guilty of an offence if—*
>
> > *(a) he intends thereby to stir up racial hatred, or*
> >
> > *(b) having regard to all the circumstances (and, in particular, taking the performance as a whole) racial hatred is likely to be stirred up thereby.*
>
> *(2) If a person presenting or directing the performance is not shown to have intended to stir up racial hatred, it is a defence for him to prove—*
>
> > *(a) that he did not know and had no reason to suspect that the performance would involve the use of the offending words or behaviour, or*

(b) that he did not know and had no reason to suspect that the offending words or behaviour were threatening, abusive or insulting, or

(c) that he did not know and had no reason to suspect that the circumstances in which the performance would be given would be such that racial hatred would be likely to be stirred up.

(3) This section does not apply to a performance given solely or primarily for one or more of the following purposes—

(a) rehearsal,

(b) making a recording of the performance, or

(c) enabling the performance to be included in a programme service;

but if it is proved that the performance was attended by persons other than those directly connected with the giving of the performance or the doing in relation to it of the things mentioned in paragraph (b) or (c), the performance shall, unless the contrary is shown, be taken not to have been given solely or primarily for the purposes mentioned above.

(4) For the purposes of this section—

(a) a person shall not be treated as presenting a performance of a play by reason only of his taking part in it as a performer,

(b) a person taking part as a performer in a performance directed by another shall be treated as a person who directed the performance if without reasonable excuse he performs otherwise than in accordance with that person's direction, and

(c) a person shall be taken to have directed a performance of a play given under his direction notwithstanding that he was not present during the performance; and a person shall not be treated

as aiding or abetting the commission of an offence under this section by reason only of his taking part in a performance as a performer.

(5) In this section "play" and "public performance" have the same meaning as in the Theatres Act 1968.

(6) The following provisions of the Theatres Act 1968 apply in relation to an offence under this section as they apply to an offence under section 2 of that Act—

section 9 (script as evidence of what was performed),

section 10 (power to make copies of script),

section 15 (powers of entry and inspection)."

Section 29D states:

"***29D. Public performance of play***

(1) If a public performance of a play is given which involves the use of threatening words or behaviour, any person who presents or directs the performance is guilty of an offence if he intends thereby to stir up religious hatred or hatred on the grounds of sexual orientation.

(2) This section does not apply to a performance given solely or primarily for one or more of the following purposes—

(a) rehearsal,

(b) making a recording of the performance, or

(c) enabling the performance to be included in a programme service;

but if it is proved that the performance was attended by persons other than those directly connected with the giving of the performance or the doing in relation to it of the things mentioned in paragraph (b) or (c), the performance shall, unless the contrary is shown, be taken not to have been given solely or primarily for the purpose mentioned above.

(3) For the purposes of this section—

(a) a person shall not be treated as presenting a performance of a play by reason only of his taking part in it as a performer,

(b) a person taking part as a performer in a performance directed by another shall be treated as a person who directed the performance if without reasonable excuse he performs otherwise than in accordance with that person's direction, and

(c) a person shall be taken to have directed a performance of a play given under his direction notwithstanding that he was not present during the performance;

and a person shall not be treated as aiding or abetting the commission of an offence under this section by reason only of his taking part in a performance as a performer.

(4) In this section "play" and "public performance" have the same meaning as in the Theatres Act 1968.

(5) The following provisions of the Theatres Act 1968 apply in relation to an offence under this section as they apply to an offence under section 2 of that Act—

section 9 (script as evidence of what was performed),

section 10 (power to make copies of script),

section 15 (powers of entry and inspection)."

Elements of the Offences

Under both sections 20 and 29D of the 1986 Act, the Prosecution will need to prove:

i. That there was public performance of a play;

ii. That it involved the use of threatening, or (in the case of section 20 only) abusive or insulting, words or behaviour;

iii. That the defendant presented or directed the performance;

iv. That the defendant intended thereby to stir up racial hatred or hatred on the grounds of religion or sexual orientation; or

v. In the case of section 20 only, that having regard to all the circumstances (and, in particular, taking the performance as a whole) racial hatred is likely to be stirred up thereby.

Section 20 provides that the defendant may not only commit the offence if he intended to stir up racial hatred, but that it may also be committed if racial hatred is likely to be stirred up (in common with sections 18 and 19). There is no comparable provision in section 29D. Where the Prosecution bring the case on that basis, there is a statutory defence under section 20(2), if the defendant can show:

i. That he did not know, and had no reason to suspect, that the performance would involve the use of the offending words or behaviour; or

ii. That he did not know, and had no reason to suspect, that the offending words or behaviour were threatening, abusive or insulting; or

iii. That he did not know, and had no reason to suspect, that the circumstances in which the performance would be given would be such that racial hatred would be likely to be stirred up.

In order to commit the offence, the performance of the play must be a public performance. Both sections state that 'play' and 'public performance' are to have the same meaning as in the Theatres Act 1968. Under the Theatres Act 1968, 'play' is defined as follows:

> " *'play' means—*
>
> *(a) any dramatic piece, whether involving improvisation or not, which is given wholly or in part by one or more persons actually present and performing and in which the whole or a major proportion of what is done by the person or persons performing, whether by way of speech, singing or action, involves the playing of a role; and*
>
> *(b) any ballet given wholly or in part by one or more persons actually present and performing, whether or not it falls within paragraph (a) of this definition;*"

Under the same Act, 'public performance' is defined as follows:

> " *"public performance" includes any performance in a public place within the meaning of the Public Order Act 1936 and any performance which the public or any section thereof are permitted to attend, whether on payment or otherwise;*"

Sections 20 and 29D then provide additional exceptions to the application of the offence. The section will not apply to a performance given solely or primarily for a) a rehearsal; b) making a recording of the performance; or c) enabling the performance to be included in a programme service.

Note that those exceptions only apply where they were the sole or primary reason for the performance. Both sections of the legislation clarify that, where it is proved that where the performance was attended by people who were not directly connected with giving the performance (e.g. actors), or with making the recording or enabling the performance to be included in a programme service (e.g. videographers) then the performance will be taken not to have been given solely or primarily for the exceptional purposes. For example, a rehearsal open to members of the public will be presumed not to have been given solely or primarily for rehearsal purposes. The defendant can rebut this presumption where it is shown that, despite the attendance of those people, the performance was given solely or primarily for the purposes allowed.

Sections 20(4) and 29D(3) assist with our interpretation of who might be considered to have presented or directed a performance. In summary:

i. A person is not to be treated as 'presenting' a play simply because he performed in that play;

ii. However, if that person acts otherwise than in accordance with the direction of the person directing the play, without reasonable excuse, he then shall be treated as a person who directed the performance;

iii. If a play takes part under a person's direction, that person is to be taken as having directed the play, even if he was not present during the performance;

iv. Additionally, a person who performs in a play shall not be treated as aiding or abetting the commission of an offence under sections 19 or 29D simply because he performed in that play.

Therefore, a person who simply acts in a play will not have committed an offence under sections 19 or 29D. Additionally, he will not be taken as to have aided or abetted an offence. However, this is not a blanket protection; if that performer then acts on his own initiative and uses words or behaviour that contravene the provisions of the section, then he is treated as a director, and so sections 19 and 29D apply to him. This helps to ensure that directors are not convicted on the basis of rogue actions of their performers. Finally, these provisions ensure that a director cannot escape criminal liability simply because he is not physically present during the performance; if the play takes part under his direction, then that is sufficient to treat him as a director.

Sections 21 and 29E of the Public Order Act 1986

Sections 21 and 29E create offences in relation to distributing, showing or playing a recording. Section 20 creates an offence in relation to racial hatred. Section 29E creates a like offence in relation to hatred on the grounds of religion or sexual orientation.

Section 21 states:

> "***21. Distributing, showing or playing a recording.***
>
> *(1) A person who distributes, or shows or plays, a recording of visual images or sounds which are threatening, abusive or insulting is guilty of an offence if—*
>
> *(a) he intends thereby to stir up racial hatred, or*
>
> *(b) having regard to all the circumstances racial hatred is likely to be stirred up thereby.*
>
> *(2) In this Part "recording" means any record from which visual images or sounds may, by any means, be reproduced; and references to the distribution, showing or playing of a recording are to its distribution, showing or playing of a recording are to its distribution, showing or playing to the public or a section of the public.*
>
> *(3) In proceedings for an offence under this section it is a defence for an accused who is not shown to have intended to stir up racial hatred to prove that he was not aware of the content of the recording and did not suspect, and had no reason to suspect, that it was threatening, abusive or insulting.*

(4) This section does not apply to the showing or playing of a recording solely for the purpose of enabling the recording to be included in a programme service."

Section 29E states:

"***29E. Distributing, showing or playing a recording***

(1) A person who distributes, or shows or plays, a recording of visual images or sounds which are threatening is guilty of an offence if he intends thereby to stir up religious hatred or hatred on the grounds of sexual orientation.

(2) In this Part "recording" means any record from which visual images or sounds may, by any means, be reproduced; and references to the distribution, showing or playing of a recording are to its distribution, showing or playing to the public or a section of the public.

(3) This section does not apply to the showing or playing of a recording solely for the purpose of enabling the recording to be included in a programme service."

Elements of the Offences

Under both sections 21 and 29E of the 1986 Act, the Prosecution will need to prove:

i. That the defendant distributed, showed or played a recording of visual images or sounds;

ii. That the visual images or sounds were threatening or (in the case of section 21 only) abusive or insulting;

iii. That the defendant intended thereby to stir up racial hatred or hatred on the grounds of religion or sexual orientation; or

iv. Under section 21 only, that, having regard to all the circumstances, racial hatred was likely to be stirred up thereby.

Sections 21(2) and 29E(2) define recording and distribution. By virtue of that definition, distribution means its distribution, showing or playing to the public or to a section of the public. It is not, however, an offence where the recording is showed or played solely for the purposes of enabling it to be included in a programme service. Under section 29 of the 1986 Act, 'programme service' has the same meaning as in the Broadcasting Act 1990. Section 201 of the Broadcasting Act 1990 defines 'programme service'. Its provisions are detailed, and do not warrant a great deal of analysis here, but in summary, a programme service is (whether or not it requires a licence):

i. Any service which is a programme service within the meaning of the Communications Act 2003;

ii. Any other service that consists in the sending, by means of an electronic communication, sounds or visual images or both for a) reception at two or more places in the United Kingdom; b) reception at a place in the United Kingdom for the purpose of being presented there to members of the public or any group of persons.

There are specific caveats added to the latter term under that section.

Section 21 alone provides that the offence might be committed even where the defendant did not intend to stir up racial hatred but, having regard to all the circumstances, racial hatred was likely to be stirred up thereby. In common with preceding provisions, then, section 21 provides a statutory defence where the Prosecution relies upon the allegation that racial hatred was likely to be stirred up, rather than proving intent. The defendant has a statutory defence if he can prove that he was not aware of the content of the recording and did not suspect, nor had reason to suspect, that it was threatening, abusive or insulting. This would apply, then, to someone who had simply distributed another person's recording, without listening to it or watching it themselves, and who had no suspicion that it would be threatening, abusive or insulting. An example of the use of such a defence might be where the accused is a web technician employed to distribute a video recording through the Internet, with no knowledge of the content of the recording, nor any suspicion of his employer's racially hostile views.

Sections 22 and 29F of the Public Order Act 1986

Sections 22 and 29F create offences relating to broadcasting or including a programme in a cable programme service. Section 22 creates offences in relation to racial hatred. Section 29F creates a similar offence in relation to religious hatred, or hatred on the grounds of sexual orientation.

Section 22 states:

> "***22. Broadcasting or including programme in cable programme service.***
>
> *(1) If a programme involving threatening, abusive or insulting visual images or sounds is included in a programme service, each of the persons mentioned in subsection (2) is guilty of an offence if—*
>
> > *(a) he intends thereby to stir up racial hatred, or*
> >
> > *(b) having regard to all the circumstances racial hatred is likely to be stirred up thereby.*
>
> *(2) The persons are—*
>
> > *(a) the person providing the programme service,*
> >
> > *(b) any person by whom the programme is produced or directed, and*
> >
> > *(c) any person by whom offending words or behaviour are used.*

(3) If the person providing the service, or a person by whom the programme was produced or directed, is not shown to have intended to stir up racial hatred, it is a defence for him to prove that—

(a) he did not know and had no reason to suspect that the programme would involve the offending material, and

(b) having regard to the circumstances in which the programme was included in a programme service, it was not reasonably practicable for him to secure the removal of the material.

(4) It is a defence for a person by whom the programme was produced or directed who is not shown to have intended to stir up racial hatred to prove that he did not know and had no reason to suspect—

(a) that the programme would be included in a programme service, or

(b) that the circumstances in which the programme would be so included would be such that racial hatred would be likely to be stirred up.

(5) It is a defence for a person by whom offending words or behaviour were used and who is not shown to have intended to stir up racial hatred to prove that he did not know and had no reason to suspect—

(a) that a programme involving the use of the offending material would be included in a programme service, or

(b) that the circumstances in which a programme involving the use of the offending material would be so included, or in which a programme so included would involve the use of the offending material, would be such that racial hatred would be likely to be stirred up.

(6) A person who is not shown to have intended to stir up racial hatred is not guilty of an offence under this section if he did not

> *know, and had no reason to suspect, that the offending material was threatening, abusive or insulting.*"

Section 29F states:

> "***29F. Broadcasting or including programme in programme service***
>
> *(1) If a programme involving threatening visual images or sounds is included in a programme service, each of the persons mentioned in subsection (2) is guilty of an offence if he intends thereby to stir up religious hatred or hatred on the grounds of sexual orientation.*
>
> *(2) The persons are—*
>
> *(a) the person providing the programme service,*
>
> *(b) any person by whom the programme is produced or directed, and*
>
> *(c) any person by whom offending words or behaviour are used.*"

Elements of the Offence

In order to prove an offence under sections 22 or 29F of the 1986 Act, the Prosecution will need to prove:

i. That the programme in question was included in a programme service;

ii. That the programme involved threatening or (in the case of section 22 only) abusive or insulting visual images or sounds;

iii. That the defendant intended thereby to stir up racial hatred; or

iv. In the case of an offence under section 22 only, that racial hatred is likely to be stirred up thereby, having regard to all the circumstances.

Sections 22(2) and 29F(2), though, provide that only certain people might be held criminally liable under their provisions. These are:

i. The person providing the programme service;

ii. Any person by whom the programme is produced or directed; and

iii. Any person by whom offending words or behaviour are used.

Section 22 provides an extra method of committing the offence, as compared to section 29F. Under section 22, an offence is committed even where the defendant did not intend to stir up racial hatred, provided that – in all the circumstances – racial hatred is likely to be stirred up thereby. There is no comparative route to conviction in section 29F; to be convicted under that provision, the defendant must be shown to have intended that hatred based on religion or sexual orientation be stirred up.

Section 22, then, provides four statutory defences where intention is not proven. Under section 22(3), it is a defence for the defendant to prove that a) he did not know nor had reason to suspect that the programme would involve the offending material; and b) having regard to the circumstances in which the programme was included in the programme service, it was not reasonably practicable for him to secure the removal of the material. An example might be where the producer of the programme had no reason to suspect that the programme would involve racially hostile language, and when it was aired – and he did realise – it was not reasonably practicable to take the programme off the air.

Under section 22(4), it is a defence for the defendant to show that he did not know nor had reason to suspect a) that the programme would be included in a programme service; or b) that the circumstances in which the programme would be so included would be such that racial hatred would be likely to be stirred up. An example might be where a person used offending words or behaviour whilst being filmed, with no reason to suspect that it would be aired.

Under section 22(5), the defendant is not guilty if he proves that he did not know, nor had reason to suspect, that a programme involving the use of offending material would be included in a programme service; or b) that the circumstances in which a programme involving the use of offending material would be included would be such that racial hatred would be likely to be stirred up. An example might be where the person providing the programme service had no reason to suspect that a racially hostile programme would be included in that service.

Finally, under section 22(6), the defendant is not guilty if he did not know, and had no reason to suspect, that the offending material was threatening, abusive or insulting.

Sections 23 and 29G of the Public Order Act 1986

Section 23 of the 1986 Act creates an offence of possession of racially inflammatory material. Section 29G creates a like offence in relation to material that is inflammatory on the grounds of religious hatred and hatred on the grounds of sexual orientation.

Section 23 states:

> "***23. Possession of racially inflammatory material.***
>
> *(1) A person who has in his possession written material which is threatening, abusive or insulting, or a recording of visual images or sounds which are threatening, abusive or insulting, with a view to—*

(a) in the case of written material, its being displayed, published, distributed, or included in a cable programme service, whether by himself or another, or

(b) in the case of a recording, its being distributed, shown, played, or included in a cable programme service, whether by himself or another,

is guilty of an offence if he intends racial hatred to be stirred up thereby or, having regard to all the circumstances, racial hatred is likely to be stirred up thereby.

(2) For this purpose regard shall be had to such display, publication, distribution, showing, playing, or inclusion in a programme service as he has, or it may reasonably be inferred that he has, in view.

(3) In proceedings for an offence under this section it is a defence for an accused who is not shown to have intended to stir up racial hatred to prove that he was not aware of the content of the written material or recording and did not suspect, and had no reason to suspect, that it was threatening, abusive or insulting".

Section 29G states:

"***29G. Possession of inflammatory material***

(1) A person who has in his possession written material which is threatening, or a recording of visual images or sounds which are threatening, with a view to—

(a) in the case of written material, its being displayed, published, distributed, or included in a programme service whether by himself or another, or

(b) in the case of a recording, its being distributed, shown, played, or included in a programme service, whether by himself or

another, is guilty of an offence if he intends thereby to stir up religious hatred or hatred on the grounds of sexual orientation.

(2) For this purpose regard shall be had to such display, publication, distribution, showing, playing, or inclusion in a programme service as he has, or it may reasonably be inferred that he has, in view."

Elements of the Offence

Essentially, sections 23 and 29G create offences of possessing written material or recordings that are intended to be used to commit an offence under one of the preceding sections.

In order to prove an offence under sections 23 or 29G of the 1986 Act, the Prosecution will need to prove:

i. The defendant had written material or a recording of visual images or sounds in their possession;

ii. That material or recording was threatening or (in the case of section 23 only) abusive or insulting;

iii. In the case of written material, the defendant intended that the material be distributed, shown, played or included in a programme service, whether by the defendant or another person; or

iv. In the case of a recording, the defendant intended that it be distributed, shown, played or included in a programme service, whether by the defendant or another person;

v. The defendant intended racial hatred or hatred on the grounds of religion or sexual orientation to be stirred up thereby; or

vi. In the case of section 23 only, having regard to all the circumstances, racial hatred is likely to be stirred up thereby.

Sections 29 (applying to offences created by sections 18 to 23) and 29N (applying to offences created by sections 29B to 29G) of the 1986 Act define 'written material' as "*any sign or other visible representation*".

As with previous provisions, it is possible to prove the racially aggravated form either by proving intent on the part of the defendant, or because – having regard to all the circumstances – racial hatred is likely to be stirred up by the offending action. Section 23 therefore provides a statutory defence where the case is not put on the basis of intent. Under section 23(3), it is a defence for an accused to prove that he was not aware of the content of the written material or recording and did not suspect, nor had reason to suspect, that it was threatening, abusive or insulting. It is, then, not enough for the defendant to simply say that he was not aware of the content of the material. He will only be able to avail himself of the defence if he can positively show that he not only lacked awareness of the material's content, but had no reason to suspect the nature of the content; a person who has wilfully closed his eyes to the content of the material will not be able to escape criminal liability. We can imagine, therefore, that it will be largely those on the periphery of matters – effectively, those acting as couriers – who will be able to avail themselves of the statutory defence.

Sections 23(2) and 29G(2) provide that regard shall be had to such display, publication, distribution, showing, playing or inclusion in a programme service that the defendant has, or it may be reasonably inferred that he has, in view. In other words, then, when considering whether the defendant has a view to publication, and whether he intends to stir up hatred, the form of display, publication etc that the Court should consider will be the actual one that the defendant had in mind, or one that reasonable inference indicates that he had in mind. This will prevent the Court drawing conclusions based upon other forms of display, publication etc than that which was actually to be used.

The Football Offences Act 1991

The relevant provision in the Football Offences Act 1991 ("the 1991 Act") is section 3. That creates an offence of indecent or racialist chanting at a football match, as follows:

> "***3. Indecent or racialist chanting.***
>
> *(1) It is an offence to engage or take part in chanting of an indecent or racialist nature at a designated football match.*
>
> *(2) For this purpose—*
>
> > *(a) "chanting" means the repeated uttering of any words or sounds (whether alone or in concert with one more others)]; and*
> >
> > *(b) "of a racialist nature" means consisting of or including matter which is threatening, abusive or insulting to a person by reason of his colour, race, nationality (including citizenship) or ethnic or national origins."*

Elements of the Offence

In order to prove the offence, the Prosecution need to prove:

i. That the person engaged or took part in chanting;

ii. The chanting was of an indecent or racialist nature;

iii. The chanting was at a designated football match;

'Chanting' is defined in section 3 as the repeated uttering of words or sounds. Even doing so alone can constitute chanting; it need not be in concert with others.

'Of a racialist nature' is defined in section 3 and repeats concepts with which we are now familiar. It is defined as either consisting of or including matter which is threatening, abusive or insulting to a person by reason of his colour, race, nationality (including citizenship) or ethnic or national origins. The wording of that definition does not require that there be a 'victim' in the same way as the 'demonstration' limb of the 1998 Act, nor does it require a person to be specifically targeted. It simply requires that the words be threatening, abusive or insulting to a person by reason of his colour, etc.

Once again, we see that 'race' does not simply encompass a person's race for the purposes of the offence. It also encompasses his colour, nationality (including citizenship), or ethnic or national origins. In this way, it mimics the wording within other statutes.

Section 1 of the 1991 Act provides assistance as to the meaning of a 'designated football match'. By section 1(1), a 'designated football match' means:

> "*...an association football match designated, or of a description designated, for the purposes of this Act by order of the Secretary of State. Any such order shall be made by statutory instrument which shall be subject to annulment in pursuance of a resolution of either House of Parliament.*"

Section 3 does not just apply to chanting that occurs during the period of the football match itself. By virtue of section 1(2) of the 1991 Act, references to things done at a designated football match include anything done at the ground a) within the period beginning two hours before the start of the match or (if earlier) two hours before the time at which it is advertised to start, and ending one hour after the end of the match; or b) where the match is advertised to start at a particular time on a particular day but does not in fact take place on that day, within the period beginning two hours before and ending one hour after the advertised start time. Therefore, racialist chanting before or after the football match will still be an offence under this section, provided it takes place at the ground, and is within the designated time period.

Of course, sporting events such as football can stoke rivalries between competing teams and, therefore, people from different cities; a certain amount of good-humoured insult can be accepted. It does not follow that racist language or behaviour can find itself tolerated. In *DPP v Stoke on Trent Magistrates' Court* [2003] EWHC 1593 (Admin), the appeal centred on whether certain words reached the standard of criminality, or were mere 'doggerel', and amounted to no more than to say 'our town is better than your town'. In that case, the DPP appealed by way of case stated against a District Judge's decision to acquit the Respondent on a charge under section 3 of the 1991 Act. The Respondent, a Port Vale supporter, had directed the group chant "*you're just a town full of Pakis*" at fans from Oldham. The District Judge had found that the phrase was 'mere doggerel', amounting to no more than a statement that 'our town is better than your town' and that 'Pakis' was a mere shortening of the word 'Pakistani' and no more racialist than the use of the words 'Brit' or "Yank'. Allowing the DPP's appeal, it was held that 'Paki' was commonly understood to be racially offensive. The use of the word had to be examined in the context of each case, but there was no doubt that the Respondent had used it in a racially derogatory and insulting sense.

Offences Against Ministers and Places of Worship

Finally, there are two offences that find their way into this book because they are targeted at people and places linked closely with religion. Many criminal practitioners will be far more likely to come across the previous offences discussed than these. However, it is worth being aware of them.

Section 2 of the Ecclesiastical Courts Jurisdiction Act 1860

Section 2 of the Ecclesiastical Courts Jurisdiction Act 1860 states:

"2. Penalty on persons found guilty of making a disturbance in churches, chapels, churchyards, or burial grounds.

Any person who shall be guilty of riotous, violent, or indecent behaviour in England or Ireland in any cathedral church, parish or district church or chapel of the Church of England, or in any chapel of any religious denomination, or in England in any places of religious worship duly certified under the provisions of the Places of Worship Registration Act 1855 , whether during the celebration of divine service or at any other time, or in any churchyard or burial ground, or who shall molest, let, disturb, vex, or trouble, or by any other unlawful means disquiet or misuse any preacher duly authorized to preach therein, or any clergyman in holy orders ministering or celebrating any sacrament, or any divine service, rite, or office, in any cathedral, church, or chapel, or in any churchyard or burial ground, shall, on conviction thereof by a magistrates' court, be liable to a fine not exceeding level 1 on the standard scale or to imprisonment for a term not exceeding two months."

In other words, section 2 makes it an offence to carry out 'riotous, violent or indecent' behaviour in a church or chapel in England or Ireland. It also makes it an offence to 'disquiet or misuse' a preacher or a clergyman when they are performing their religious duties in a cathedral, church, chapel, churchyard or burial ground.

The offence is a summary only offence, and the maximum penalty is a term of two months' imprisonment.

<u>Section 36 of the Offences Against the Person Act 1861</u>

Section 36 of the Offences Against the Person Act 1861 states:

"36. Obstructing or assaulting a clergyman or other minister in the discharge of his duties.

> *Whosoever shall, by threats or force, obstruct or prevent or endeavour to obstruct or prevent, any clergyman or other minister in or from celebrating divine service or otherwise officiating in any church, chapel, meeting house, or other place of divine worship, or in or from the performance of his duty in the lawful burial of the dead in any churchyard or other burial place, or shall strike or offer any violence to, or shall, upon any civil process, or under the pretence of executing any civil process, arrest any clergyman or other minister who is engaged in, or to the knowledge of the offender is about to engage in, any of the rites or duties in this section aforesaid, or who to the knowledge of the offender shall be going to perform the same or returning from the performance thereof, shall be guilty of a misdemeanor, and being convicted thereof shall be liable, at the discretion of the court, to be imprisoned for any term not exceeding two years"*

This section makes it an offence to use threats or force in order to obstruct or prevent, or try to obstruct or prevent, a clergyman or other minister from officiating in – essentially – their official duties within the church, chapel, meeting house or 'other place of divine worship'. This includes the lawful burial of the dead. The offence is triable either way, and the maximum penalty on conviction is two years' imprisonment.

CHAPTER FIVE
THE SENTENCING UPLIFT PROVISIONS

This chapter discusses the sentencing uplift provisions in sections 145 and 146 of the Criminal Justice Act 2003. It considers the application of these provisions by reference to relevant caselaw.

As discussed in Chapter Two, the law of hate crime in the United Kingdom can be divided into two strands: 1) statutory offences; 2) the sentencing uplift. In Chapter Four, we considered the statutory offences in some detail. Where the evidence points towards the commission of one of those statutory offences, it will be that which finds its way to the charge sheet or Indictment.

However, relying on the statutory offences alone would leave some gaping deficiencies in the goal to tackle hate-based offending. First, there are a number of basic offences that are not complemented by an aggravated alternative. For example, no theft offences have aggravated versions. Robbery requires the use or threat of violence; we can relatively quickly contemplate situations in which the violence element is to some extent motivated by hostility based on one of the protected characteristics. Secondly, the statutory offences largely create racial and religious hate crimes, albeit there is some creation of homophobic hate crimes in the Public Order Act 1986. Therefore, transphobic crimes, hate crimes against disabled people and (to a large extent) homophobic crimes are not catered for.

Sections 145 and 146 of the Criminal Justice Act 2003 address these gaps with 'blanket' provisions that apply to all offences. These two provisions give the Court the duty to increase the sentence for a defendant who has either demonstrated, or been motivated by, hostility based on the victim's race, religion, sexual orientation, disability or transgender identity (or the defendant's presumption that the victim has any of those characteristics).

It is important to note that sections 145 and 146 of the 2003 Act apply at the sentencing stage. Unlike the statutory offences set out in Chapter Four, the aggravation is not an element of the offence to be proven for conviction. Therefore, the jury or magistrates hearing the trial need only make the decision as to whether the elements of the simple offence are proven. It is for the sentencing Judge or Magistrate to determine whether the requisite aggravation was present when the offence was committed. If the Sentencing Judge or Magistrate makes a positive determination, then the duty to treat that as an aggravating factor is triggered.

Where there has been a trial, the sentencing Judge or Magistrates should often have adjudicated the trial. In those circumstances, they will have heard evidence of the circumstances in which the offence took place, and can draw their conclusions based upon that.

Where there has not been a trial, due to a guilty plea, and the Prosecution claims that the uplift is applicable, the Judge or Magistrates will need to determine whether the evidence supports that submission. It is extremely likely that, where the defendant disputes the facts that are said to lead to the aggravation, a Newton Hearing (i.e. a trial of a specific disputed factual issue at sentencing stage) will be necessary to decide this point. A Newton hearing should be held where the decision on the disputed area is likely to make a significant difference to sentence. Given that the effect of a positive finding under sections 145 or 146 is that the offence must be further aggravated, it is difficult to envisage a situation where the defence dispute the facts that are said to amount to the aggravation, and yet a Newton hearing is not appropriate. Indeed, this was the conclusion of the Divisional Court in *DPP v Giles* [2019] EWHC 2015 (Admin). It is submitted, though, that where there is no dispute that the relevant action took place, but the dispute simply centres around whether that action evidences the requisite hostility (e.g. whether a certain word used amounts to a slur), it may well be more useful to invite submissions of the advocates as to the interpretation that the Court should adopt than to call live evidence by way of a Newton hearing. Even in those circumstances, though, the live evidence might assist in determining the context in which the actions took place, and so informing the proper interpretation.

Section 145 of the Criminal Justice Act 2003

Section 145 of the 2003 Act creates a sentencing uplift for offences where the Court finds that there was racial or religious aggravation.

Section 145 states:

> "***145. Increase in sentences for racial or religious aggravation***
>
> *(1) This section applies where a court is considering the seriousness of an offence other than one under sections 29 to 32 of the Crime and Disorder Act 1998 (c. 37) (racially or religiously aggravated assaults, criminal damage, public order offences and harassment etc).*
>
> *(2) If the offence was racially or religiously aggravated, the court—*
>
> > *(a) must treat that fact as an aggravating factor, and*
> >
> > *(b) must state in open court that the offence was so aggravated.*
>
> *(3) Section 28 of the Crime and Disorder Act 1998 (meaning of "racially or religiously aggravated") applies for the purposes of this section as it applies for the purposes of sections 29 to 32 of that Act.*"

Application of section 145 of the Criminal Justice Act 2003

Section 145 of the 2003 Act applies to any offences that are not already provided for by sections 29 to 32 of the Crime and Disorder Act 1998 (see Chapter Four). There is no need for a separate sentencing uplift where one of those offences is charged; sections 29 to 32 explicitly provide greater sentences than their basic counterparts.

Section 145 refers us to section 28 of the Crime and Disorder Act 1998 for the meaning of 'racially or religiously aggravated' (see Chapter 3 for a detailed discussion of these provisions).

Under section 145(2), where the Court determines that the offence was racially or religiously aggravated, the Court is not only obliged to treat it as an aggravating factor, but to state in open court that the offence is aggravated.

Where there are multiple offences on an Indictment, or charge sheet, the Court must consider each separately to determine whether each is aggravated. It may be that two concurrent offences warrant separate conclusions as to whether they are aggravated or not. In *Channon* [2011] EWCA Crim 1861, the appellant had held a knife to a Muslim man outside a mosque during an altercation about the parking of a bicycle. When the complainant threatened to call the police, the appellant slapped him and used the word 'Taliban'. At court, the appellant pleaded guilty to racially aggravated assault by beating (or common assault) and to possession of a bladed article, on the basis that he had the knife on him legitimately but then produced the knife out of fear of the complainant. He was sentenced to eight months' imprisonment for the aggravated assault, and 16 months' imprisonment for possession of a bladed article. The Judge found that the bladed article offence was racially aggravated for the purposes of section 145 of the 2003 Act. In allowing the appeal against sentence for the bladed article, the Court of Appeal held that the Judge was wrong in holding that section 145 of the 2003 Act applied to the bladed article, notwithstanding the fact that there was no dispute that the assault in the same incident was racially aggravated.

Channon, *supra*, also reminds us that to prove demonstration of hostility, there must be a victim against whom the hostility is demonstrated. In that case, Possession of a Bladed Article could not be said to be an offence with a victim; the offence is complete simply once possession without reasonable excuse is proven.

The Court is entitled to look at the offence as a whole when determining whether it is aggravated. In *Cooke* [2015] EWCA Crim 1414, the Judge was entitled to find that the appellant's actions had been aggravated by religious hostility, when – as an English Defence League member – he had joined in violence against largely Asian demonstrators and had taken part in violence that was clearly motivated by Anti-Muslim sentiment. The fact that there was no evidence to say that he himself had taken part in, for example, anti-Muslim chanting did not stop the sentencing Judge reaching the conclusion that, given all the circumstances, the offence was aggravated by religious hostility.

Where a statutory aggravated version of the offence is available, but only the basic version has been charged, it is open to the sentencing Judge to find that the offence is aggravated under section 145 of the 2003 Act and sentence accordingly. However, this power should not allow Prosecutors to escape their duty to charge the most appropriate offence; where there is evidence of a statutory aggravated offence, that should be the one charged (*O'Leary* [2015] EWCA Crim 1306).

Section 146 of the Criminal Justice Act 2003

Section 146 of the 2003 Act creates a sentencing uplift for offences where the Court finds that there was aggravation on the basis of disability, sexual orientation or transgender identity.

Section 146 states:

"146. Increase in sentences for aggravation related to disability, sexual orientation or transgender identity

(1) This section applies where the court is considering the seriousness of an offence committed in any of the circumstances mentioned in subsection (2).

(2) Those circumstances are—

(a) that, at the time of committing the offence, or immediately before or after doing so, the offender demonstrated towards the victim of the offence hostility based on—

(i) the sexual orientation (or presumed sexual orientation) of the victim,

(ii) a disability (or presumed disability) of the victim, or

(iii) the victim being (or being presumed to be) transgender, or

(b) that the offence is motivated (wholly or partly)—

(i) by hostility towards persons who are of a particular sexual orientation,

(ii) by hostility towards persons who have a disability or a particular disability, or

(iii) by hostility towards persons who are transgender.

(3) The court—

(a) must treat the fact that the offence was committed in any of those circumstances as an aggravating factor, and

(b) must state in open court that the offence was committed in such circumstances.

(4) It is immaterial for the purposes of paragraph (a) or (b) of sub-section (2) whether or not the offender's hostility is also based, to any extent, on any other factor not mentioned in that paragraph.

(5) In this section "disability" means any physical or mental impairment.

(6) In this section references to being transgender include references to being transsexual, or undergoing, proposing to undergo or having undergone a process or part of a process of gender reassignment."

Application of section 146 of the Criminal Justice Act 2003

Section 146 creates the same powers for the Court as section 145, but in relation to offences motivated by, or demonstrating, hostility based on sexual orientation, disability or transgender identity.

Section 146(2)(a) states that this provision applies to offences where at the time of committing the offence, or immediately before or after doing so, the offender demonstrated towards the victim hostility based on (i) sexual orientation (or presumed sexual orientation) of the victim; (ii) disability (or presumed disability) of the victim; or (iii) the victim being (or presumed to be) transgender. This mirrors the wording of section 28 of the 1998 Act, in relation to religious and racial aggravation. As with that provision, in order for hostility to be demonstrated, there must be a victim against whom it is demonstrated.

Again, there is no requirement to prove that the victim is of a certain sexual orientation, has a disability or is transgender; it is enough to prove that the defendant presumed that the victim had any of those characteristics.

Section 146(2)(b) states that the provision applies to offences that are motivated, wholly or partly, by hostility towards people (i) of a particular sexual orientation; (ii) who have a disability or particular disability; or (iii) who are transgender. Section 146(2)(b)(ii) makes it clear that the defendant need not be motivated by hostility towards all people with a disability, but their hostility might be targeted towards those with a particular disability.

Where the conditions of either sections 146(2)(a) or 146(2)(b) are satisfied, section 146(3) imposes a duty on the Court to treat the fact that the offence was committed in any of those circumstances as an aggravating factor, and to state as such in open Court.

As with the provisions relating to racial and religious aggravation in the 1998 Act, the defendant's hostility need not be based solely, or even primarily, on the protected characteristic. Section 146(4) of the 2003 Act provides that it is immaterial to a finding under that provision that the defendant's hostility was based on any other factor, "*to any extent*". Thus, the Prosecution need not be faced with the potentially difficult task of proving that the defendant's hostility was focused largely on the protected characteristic; it is sufficient to prove that it was one of the factors in the commission of the offence.

Section 146(5) clarifies that 'disability' has a broad spectrum; it refers to both physical and mental impairments. Section 146(6) defines the use of the word 'transgender': not only does it refer to being transsexual, but to all stages of the process of transformation. This includes proposing to undergo gender reassignment. So it is that those defendants demonstrating hostility towards a person based on their proposed reassignment cannot escape stronger punishment simply because their victim has not yet begun the physical process.

Hostility towards a person due to their sexual orientation exclusively refers to the gender towards which they are attracted, i.e. whether they are heterosexual, bisexual or homosexual – it does not extend further. This reflects the everyday definition of 'sexual orientation' in the Oxford English Dictionary, and to the definition in the Equality Act 2010. Thus where the offender had called someone a 'paedophile' immediately before committing the assault of which he was convicted, the use of the word 'paedophile' did not aggravate it under section 146 of the 2003 Act. (*B* [2013] EWCA Crim 291).

It should be remembered that taking advantage of a person's vulnerability is still an aggravating factor, even where the hate crime elements are not made out. So in a case where the Court could not be satisfied that the offender demonstrated hostility based on the victim's disability, or was motivated by such hostility, such as to meet the conditions of section 146 of the 2003 Act, the Judge was still entitled to treat the fact that the offender knew of the victim's vulnerability as an aggravating factor (*Bridge* [2012] EWCA Crim 2270).

CHAPTER SIX
THE PRACTITIONER'S TOOLKIT

This chapter sets out a practical, stage by stage guide for the practitioner who has been given a hate crime case. It is a toolkit for both defence and prosecution practitioners – although some advice may naturally be more particular to one or the other.

Armed now with an understanding of the history, key concepts and the law of hate crime, all that remains is for some practical information, in the form of a Practitioners' Toolkit. This chapter amalgamates practical advice for both defence and prosecution representatives, from pre-charge stage through to sentence. Naturally, though, some parts may be more applicable to one party over the other. In order to keep things clear, the sections below are divided between 'Prosecution Only', 'Defence Only' and 'Prosecution and Defence'.

Pre-Charge Stage

Advising at the Police Station

Defence Only: As we have discussed in preceding chapters, once there is evidence of a hate crime, the offender faces a far more serious punishment. This is so even where there is not a specific statutory aggravated offence, due to the enhanced sentencing duty under sections 145 and 146 of the 2003 Act. It will be imperative for defence representatives advising at the police station to understand the implications of the hate crime element being proven, and the factors needed.

Generally, evidence of a hate crime will make the offence so serious that a conditional caution will not be appropriate. In certain circumstances, though, it might be an option, although this will need to be referred to a prosecutor.

Pre-Charge Advice

Prosecution Only: You may be asked to advise the Prosecution about charge. If the evidence in the case indicates that a hate crime may have been committed, you should ensure that the case is flagged as a hate crime case. You will then need to consider what in the case provides evidence of demonstration of hostility, and / or motivation. Consider what other evidence may strengthen that, and make the requests of the police to gather that evidence as early as possible in the case. For example, what are the circumstances of the defendant's previous convictions – are any of them said to have been aggravated in the same way as the instant offence? Is there reason to think that the defendant might follow a particular ideology that is linked to hostility against certain groups?

You should also consider the evidence that is available other than that of the Complainant to prove the hate crime element, as well as the substantive element. Telephone evidence, evidence of words spoken before the event, and evidence of previous incidents may all assist when proving motivation.

First Appearance, Plea and Trial Preparation and Pre-Trial Review Hearings

Special Measures

Prosecution and Defence: 'Special measures' are a range of measures, introduced by the Youth Justice and Criminal Evidence Act 1999 ("the 1999 Act"), designed to ensure that witnesses give their best evidence in court. The First Appearance (where the case will stay in the Magistrates' Court) or the Plea and Trial Preparation Hearing (where the case is in the Crown Court), will generally be the appropriate time to alert the Court about applications for special measures. Special measures are available for both prosecution and defence witnesses who are: (i) vulnerable; or (ii) intimidated.

Vulnerable witnesses are defined by section 16 of the 1999 Act as (i) all child witnesses; and (ii) any witness whose quality of evidence is likely to be diminished because they are suffering from a mental disorder, have a significant impairment of intelligence or social functioning, or have a physical disability or disorder.

Intimidated witnesses are those suffering from fear or distress in relation to giving live evidence. Certain witnesses are considered to fall automatically into this category, such as complainants in sexual offence cases and witnesses to certain offences involving guns and knives.

Prosecution Only: Consider in advance of the First Appearance / Pre-Trial Preparation Hearing whether any of the prosecution witnesses will benefit from special measures and, if so, which measures will be applied for. Where the allegation is that of a hate crime based upon the victim's disability, note that they may be considered to fall into the 'vulnerable' category. It may be necessary to obtain further information about the nature of their disability, and to what extent special measures will be able to assist them in the witness box. Where the special measures are sought on the basis that the witness will be an 'intimidated witness', then it may be necessary to obtain more information about why the witness is afraid, and consider which special measures would be able to assist the witness. In all circumstances, though, the viewpoint of the witness should be sought. Even those who are automatically considered eligible for special measures (such as complainants in sexual offence cases) may choose not to avail themselves of the special measures on offer.

When unopposed, it may be that the application for special measures can be heard at the first substantive hearing (First Appearance for summary cases, and Plea and Trial Preparation Hearing for indictable cases). When opposed, it may be that another date will be set to hear arguments about the application. In any event, Prosecutors should lodge the application with the Court and the Defence as soon as possible.

Defence Only: Special Measures are available for defence witnesses. As things stand, the 1999 Act does not apply to defendants themselves. A more detailed discussion of the measures available to defendants is beyond the scope of this book. There is, though, scope for vulnerable defendants to avail themselves of intermediaries and some limited scope for defendants to appear via video link rather than in person, under section 33A of the 1999 Act.

For cases that remain a trial in the Magistrates' Court, the defence generally notify the Court of defence witnesses in the Preparation for Effective Trial form at First Appearance. For cases that are heard in the Crown Court, the defence will generally be directed to give notification of defence witnesses along with their defence case statement, usually around 28 days after the prosecution has served its case (the prosecution's service being 'Stage 1' and the defence response being 'Stage 2'). Should the defence anticipate applications to assist any of their witnesses, then this would be the appropriate time to notify the Court. At any event, it would be advisable to notify the Court of any such application as early as possible, to allow effective case management and avoid unnecessary delays to the trial.

Hearsay and Bad Character

Prosecution Only: At the first substantive hearing (First Appearance for summary cases, and Plea and Trial Preparation Hearing for indictable cases), the Prosecution will be required to indicate whether any bad character or hearsay applications are anticipated.

In a hate crime case, relevant bad character may assist in proving motivation. For example, evidence that the defendant has committed a recent string of assaults against people of a certain religion is likely to be relevant to the question of whether his assault in the instant case is motivated by hostility towards that religion. Similarly, evidence that the defendant is an ardent member of a well-known, right-wing group with racist, violent ideologies is likely to assist in proving that his actions against the ethnic minority victim in the instant case were motivated by racial hostility.

Before the application is made, then, you should ensure that you have as much detail as possible as to the circumstances of the relevant previous offences. The police will usually supply this information. It may not only make the material difference when it comes to the admissibility of a previous conviction, but it might assist the jury to know the relevant details when the case reaches trial.

Similarly, prosecutors should carefully consider whether hearsay applications are needed as early as possible. Even in cases where the complainant cannot or will not give evidence, and is the only person who can give live evidence as to the hostile words or actions, other evidence may be admissible through the hearsay provisions. For example, the transcript of a 999 call, or first accounts given on a police officer's body-worn footage.

Defence Only: note that previous convictions of your client may well provide evidence in themselves of hostile motivation. It will be important to be prepared for such a prospect, and act accordingly. In addition, your client's ideologies and group memberships could well become relevant in ways that they would not necessarily be for the basic version of the offence; in the case of the basic offence, the Prosecution will be focused on proving intention only so far as the mental element is concerned. Where an offence is said to be aggravated, the Prosecution may well be seeking to adduce evidence that can prove motivation;

membership of a far-right group, for example, might suddenly become far more interesting.

The defence might seek to adduce evidence of bad character of people other than the defendant. This will usually be an application that arises once the defence have received disclosure of witness's previous convictions, or any other information relevant to non-defendant's character.

Trial

Prosecution and Defence: armed with decisions as to special measures, bad character and hearsay, the trial should be able to proceed as usual. There are few novel points to raise in this section: the shape of the trial will follow the path forged for it by the law; that has been considered in detail in previous chapters.

Both sides should consider the assistance that can be given to the Judge in terms of framing legal directions, where a direction as to the aggravated element will need to be given. Has the case been put by the Prosecution on the basis that hostility has been demonstrated, or on the basis that the defendant was motivated by hostility?

In certain circumstances, it may be that the defendant wishes to plead guilty to the simple version of the offence, rather than the aggravated version. Similarly, where only a non-aggravated version is available, but the Prosecution contend that hostility was present such that an uplift would be applicable, then the defendant may wish to plead on a basis that absolves him of the aggravated element. In all such cases, the Prosecution will need to carefully consider whether such an option is suitable. The Prosecuting advocate will need to give careful consideration to the official guidance from the Crown Prosecution Service and, of course, instructions from the relevant lawyer at the Crown Prosecution Service.

Sentencing

Prosecution and Defence: At sentencing stage, the aggravated offence will attract a higher penalty than the basic version. It may be, though, that the defendant reaches sentence despite there remaining a dispute as to whether the offence is in fact aggravated.

This might happen because: a) the defendant has been convicted after trial of an offence without an aggravated counterpart, but the Prosecution submit that sections 145 or 146 of the 2003 Act apply so as to uplift the sentence; or b) the defendant has pleaded guilty to an offence without an aggravated counterpart, on the basis that section 145 or 146 of the 2003 Act do not apply, which the Prosecution dispute.

Where there is a dispute as to the evidence, it will be most likely that a Newton hearing will be needed. A Newton is needed where the difference between the prosecution and defence cases is 'substantial'. The effect of a finding that the offence is aggravated will be an increase in the sentence, so it cannot be argued that there will be no substantial difference to sentence (*DPP v Giles* [2019] EWHC 2015 (Admin)). Where the dispute is not a factual dispute, but revolves more around the interpretation of words and actions, it may be that the evidence called by the prosecution is limited to agreed written evidence. Indeed, the prosecution is not obliged to call evidence at all where the basic facts are not in dispute (*Mirza* [1993] 14 Cr App R (S) 64). However, advocates may wish to consider the assistance that understanding the context of a word or action can afford to its interpretation – it may be that the Judge is aided by hearing, and being able to question, the relevant witness live.

Prosecution Only: Prosecuting advocates have long utilised victim impact statements. These are a statement made by the victim in a case solely to address the impact of the offence upon them, and their lives.

In hate crime cases, though, Community Impact Statements may be of great assistance. These are documents that set out the concerns of a community over a certain time period. They can assist the Judge in assessing the impact upon the community of offences targeted at members of that community.

Community Impact Statements can be generic or specific. Where, for example, a community has been regularly targeted, the police might compile a generic Community Impact Statement that can be used in all hate crime cases involving that community. Where a specific crime targets a community in a significant way, it may be that a specific Community Impact Statement is the most appropriate, to capture the impact of this particular incident.

A Community Impact Statement will not be appropriate for every hate crime case. It may be more relevant in, for example, high profile cases that have significantly impacted the community, cases where the attack is upon a community rather than a particular person (e.g. a place of worship), or a community that has faced consistent targeting.

Prosecution and Defence: Finally, both advocates should recall the guidance in *Kelly and Donnelly* [2001] 2 Cr App R (S) 73. The Judge should be invited to state what the sentence would have been without the hate crime element aggravating it, and then to state what the sentence is after taking into account the hate crime aggravation (See Chapter Two for further discussion).

CONCLUSION
THE FUTURE OF HATE CRIME

Much of this book has, necessarily, focused upon the current law of hate crime in England and Wales. However, the law is not a static object and must constantly evolve to reflect changes in society. At the time of writing, a Law Commission Consultation is taking place to examine whether the protected categories should be extended to include categories such as age and gender. There is increased public awareness about the existence of hate crimes and the government's firm stance against them, thanks to a number of nationwide measures. In 2011 the National Hate Crime Awareness Week was launched. In 2018 the Government implemented a nationwide hate crime campaign to increase awareness and understanding of what constitutes a hate crime. What, then, can we imagine that the future might hold for the law of hate crime?

First, it is likely that there will continue to be discussion about the adequacy of the categories of people currently protected. We have seen that the earliest pieces of legislation focused upon racial hate crime. This was then expanded to include religious hate crime and crimes based on hostility towards a person's sexual orientation. Finally, the most recent sentencing uplift provisions encompass race, religion, sexual orientation, transgender identity and disability.

Two potential new categories, which are currently the subject of discussion, are age (specifically, older people) and gender. There are some good arguments for their inclusion. After all, there is a history of marginalisation of both communities. Having said that, the inclusion of any new group must be analysed carefully. We must ensure that the inclusion of that group does in fact meet a need within society to afford particular protection to that class of people. In particular, we must be clear that there exists evidence of crimes committed against that group of people that are either motivated by, or demonstrate, hostility towards them because of that characteristic.

Secondly, there will likely be discussion, when there are to be amendments to the law, as to whether more specific statutory offences should be created (as we have under the Crime and Disorder Act 1998, for example) or whether the amendments should be made to sentencing provisions (such as the sentencing uplift provisions in the Criminal Justice Act 2003). As we have seen, the current law is a medley of both methods. There are advantages and disadvantages to both. The advantages of creating particular offences are, for example: a) that the offender's conviction record will accurately reflect the aggravated nature of the offence; and b) the jury are involved in the question of whether the hate crime element is proven and to engage with the important issues involved. However, so far as disadvantages are concerned, great care would have to be taken to ensure that all possible offences were covered, which would be an extremely lengthy process. Once the new offences were finally enacted, we would be faced with a volume of new legislation to grapple with. This entire scene is arguably unjustifiable when we consider that much the same outcome (in terms of sentence and public awareness) can be achieved through 'blanket' provisions applying to all offences, like sections 145 and 146 of the Criminal Justice Act 2003.

Finally, I have touched upon increased public awareness. This can only be augmented in an age of social media, video sharing websites, and the concept of 'going viral' – the ability for a single thought to become shared and discussed worldwide with the click of a button. Victims or witnesses of hate crime now have the ability to speak up about their experiences to thousands of people, rather than simply those in their immediate vicinity. Information as to what constitutes a hate crime offence is readily available. There are numerous support structures online. The result of all of this is that victims may feel more confident reporting offences than in the past. In the years to come, then, we will likely see a growing trend in the number of hate crime prosecutions throughout the country.

Overall, we can expect to see growth in all areas of hate crime law: expansion of its application, and increase in its use. There is certainly scope for change to the legislation. However, that is not to underestimate how far we have already come. In only a number of decades, for example, we have moved from being a society that criminalised homosexuality to a society that criminalises homophobia. Just over two decades ago, the McPherson report forced the very institutions responsible for law enforcement to analyse their own attitudes to race relations. We now have a system where the law actually imposes greater punishments for all offences with a racist element. If the law both reflects and influences the attitudes of the society in which it operates, then the fact that we have a growing statutory framework against hate crime can only bode well. We may never be able to fully eradicate hateful prejudice from society, but having the law take a firm stance is surely a start.

MORE BOOKS BY LAW BRIEF PUBLISHING

'How to Be a Freelance Solicitor: A Practical Guide to the SRA-Regulated Freelance Solicitor Model' by Paul Bennett

'A Practical Guide to Prison Injury Claims' by Malcolm Johnson

'A Practical Guide to the Small Claims Track' by Dominic Bright

'A Practical Guide to Advising Clients at the Police Station' by Colin Stephen McKeown-Beaumont

'A Practical Guide to Antisocial Behaviour Injunctions' by Iain Wightwick

'Practical Mediation: A Guide for Mediators, Advocates, Advisers, Lawyers, and Students in Civil, Commercial, Business, Property, Workplace, and Employment Cases' by Jonathan Dingle with John Sephton

'The Mini-Pupillage Workbook' by David Boyle

'A Practical Guide to Crofting Law' by Brian Inkster

'A Practical Guide to Spousal Maintenance' by Liz Cowell

'A Practical Guide to the Law of Domain Names and Cybersquatting' by Andrew Clemson

'A Practical Guide to the Law of Gender Pay Gap Reporting' by Harini Iyengar

'A Practical Guide to the Rights of Grandparents in Children Proceedings' by Stuart Barlow

'NHS Whistleblowing and the Law' by Joseph England

'Employment Law and the Gig Economy' by Nigel Mackay & Annie Powell

'A Practical Guide to Noise Induced Hearing Loss (NIHL) Claims' by Andrew Mckie, Ian Skeate, Gareth McAloon

'An Introduction to Beauty Negligence Claims – A Practical Guide for the Personal Injury Practitioner' by Greg Almond

'Intercompany Agreements for Transfer Pricing Compliance' by Paul Sutton

'Zen and the Art of Mediation' by Martin Plowman

'A Practical Guide to the SRA Principles, Individual and Law Firm Codes of Conduct 2019 – What Every Law Firm Needs to Know' by Paul Bennett

'A Practical Guide to Adoption for Family Lawyers' by Graham Pegg

'A Practical Guide to Industrial Disease Claims' by Andrew Mckie & Ian Skeate

'A Practical Guide to Redundancy' by Philip Hyland

'A Practical Guide to Vicarious Liability' by Mariel Irvine

'A Practical Guide to Applications for Landlord's Consent and Variation of Leases' by Mark Shelton

'A Practical Guide to Relief from Sanctions Post-Mitchell and Denton' by Peter Causton

'A Practical Guide to Equity Release for Advisors' by Paul Sams

'A Practical Guide to Unlawful Eviction and Harassment' by Stephanie Lovegrove

'A Practical Guide to the Law Relating to Food' by Ian Thomas

'A Practical Guide to Financial Services Claims' by Chris Hegarty

'The Law of Houses in Multiple Occupation: A Practical Guide to HMO Proceedings' by Julian Hunt

'A Practical Guide to Unlawful Eviction and Harassment' by Stephanie Lovegrove

'A Practical Guide to Solicitor and Client Costs' by Robin Dunne

'Occupiers, Highways and Defective Premises Claims: A Practical Guide Post-Jackson – 2nd Edition' by Andrew Mckie

'A Practical Guide to Financial Ombudsman Service Claims' by Adam Temple & Robert Scrivenor

'A Practical Guide to the Law of Enfranchisement and Lease Extension' by Paul Sams

'A Practical Guide to Marketing for Lawyers – 2nd Edition' by Catherine Bailey & Jennet Ingram

'A Practical Guide to Advising Schools on Employment Law' by Jonathan Holden

'A Practical Guide to Running Housing Disrepair and Cavity Wall Claims: 2nd Edition' by Andrew Mckie & Ian Skeate

'A Practical Guide to Holiday Sickness Claims – 2nd Edition' by Andrew Mckie & Ian Skeate

'Arguments and Tactics for Personal Injury and Clinical Negligence Claims' by Dorian Williams

'A Practical Guide to QOCS and Fundamental Dishonesty' by James Bentley

'A Practical Guide to Drone Law' by Rufus Ballaster, Andrew Firman, Eleanor Clot

'A Practical Guide to Compliance for Personal Injury Firms Working With Claims Management Companies' by Paul Bennett

'A Practical Guide to the Landlord and Tenant Act 1954: Commercial Tenancies' by Richard Hayes & David Sawtell

'A Practical Guide to Dog Law for Owners and Others' by Andrea Pitt
'RTA Allegations of Fraud in a Post-Jackson Era: The Handbook – 2nd Edition' by Andrew Mckie
'RTA Personal Injury Claims: A Practical Guide Post-Jackson' by Andrew Mckie
'On Experts: CPR35 for Lawyers and Experts' by David Boyle
'An Introduction to Personal Injury Law' by David Boyle
'A Practical Guide to Claims Arising From Accidents Abroad and Travel Claims' by Andrew Mckie & Ian Skeate
'A Practical Guide to Chronic Pain Claims' by Pankaj Madan
'A Practical Guide to Claims Arising from Fatal Accidents' by James Patience
'A Practical Approach to Clinical Negligence Post-Jackson' by Geoffrey Simpson-Scott
'Employers' Liability Claims: A Practical Guide Post-Jackson' by Andrew Mckie
'A Practical Guide to Subtle Brain Injury Claims' by Pankaj Madan
'A Practical Guide to Costs in Personal Injury Cases' by Matthew Hoe
'The No Nonsense Solicitors' Practice: A Guide To Running Your Firm' by Bettina Brueggemann
'The Queen's Counsel Lawyer's Omnibus: 20 Years of Cartoons from The Times 1993-2013' by Alex Steuart Williams

These books and more are available to order online direct from the publisher at www.lawbriefpublishing.com, where you can also read free sample chapters. For any queries, contact us on 0844 587 2383 or mail@lawbriefpublishing.com.

Our books are also usually in stock at www.amazon.co.uk with free next day delivery for Prime members, and at good legal bookshops such as Wildy & Sons.

We are regularly launching new books in our series of practical day-to-day practitioners' guides. Visit our website and join our free newsletter to be kept informed and to receive special offers, free chapters, etc.

You can also follow us on Twitter at www.twitter.com/lawbriefpub.

www.ingramcontent.com/pod-product-compliance
Lightning Source LLC
LaVergne TN
LVHW022055200926
848481LV00003B/922